Strugg

MW01143852

♥ *This is a wonderful gift for people who are dealing with loss, whether old or new.*

Dr. Lo Sprague, psychotherapist

♥ *Sometimes I wish that I could be a secret book-elf, and sneak into people's homes and offices and leave special books. If I could, I'd put a copy of* **Struggling and Soaring with Angels** *into the home of every person struggling with loss and into the office of every mental health professional in America.*

John James, coauthor,
When Children Grieve, founder,
The Grief Recovery Institute

♥ *Aurora Winter's writing is powerful, honest, clear, and tender. Her personal journey from tragedy through grief to acceptance will comfort anyone suffering the loss of a loved one.*

Rick Reiff, executive editor,
Orange County Business Journal

♥ *So lyrical and powerful, the words set themselves to music.*

Brahm Wenger, feature film composer

Struggling and Soaring with Angels

♥ *Beautifully done in every way. Aurora's writing is really wonderful. My eyes got a tad moist, I will readily admit. I truly believe there is a huge audience out there for this book. Aurora never ceases to amaze me!*

> Seaton McLean,
> President, Motion Picture Production,
> Alliance-Atlantis

♥ *When I get really down and feel like the big black cloud is going to suck me in, I pick up your book and re-read it, and I find myself being raised up, and the cloud doesn't seem so big and so black. Thank you.*

> Matthew Bosman

♥ *In this compassionate, powerful diary of a wife's love and a mother's challenge, Aurora Winter chronicles her pilgrimage from suffering to strength. Her poetic narrative will heal your wounded spirit and empower you to face your sorrow.*

> Cynthia Brian, radio talk show host; author,
> *Be the Star You Are!*

Aurora Winter

♥ *As a single man, I found Aurora Winter's book an affirmation that life-changing, eternal love can happen. To know that a woman could love a man this much makes the hard road of holding out for your soul mate much easier. Few men are ever blessed with an Aurora to love them, but it's great to know it's possible.*

Lee Kyle Gaither, Vice-President, NBC

♥ *A wonderful companion for people who are grieving.*

Susan Bravo, hospice social worker

♥ *Aurora Winter has been through grief and come out of it. Her words and experiences, expressed with great insight and sensitivity, have never had greater meaning.*

Joel Kotkin,
author, *The New Geography*; contributing
writer, *The Wall Street Journal*,
The New York Times

Struggling and Soaring with Angels

Aurora Winter

Struggling and Soaring with Angels

Aurora Winter

Struggling and Soaring with Angels

Healing a Broken Heart

Aurora Winter

dandelion sky
P R E S S

DANDELION SKY PRESS

Copyright © 2003 by Aurora Winter
Published by Dandelion Sky Press
1280 Bison, Suite B9-40, Newport Beach, CA, USA 92660
Phone: 866-344-3108

Front Cover Photograph: © 2000 Yousef Khanfar
Other Photographs: Michael Kraus
Book Design: Bryce Winter
Cover Design: Manny Hidalgo
Editor: Eleanor Dugan
Passages from *The Prophet* by Kahlil Gibran used with kind
permission of Random House, Inc.

All rights reserved. This book, or parts thereof, may not be
reproduced in whole or in part without written permission
from the publisher, except by a reviewer who may quote
brief passages in a review.

Winter, Aurora.
    Struggling and soaring with angels : healing a broken
heart / Aurora Winter.
    p. cm.
    ISBN 0-9722497-8-8

    1. Grief. 2. Bereavement--Psychological aspects.
3. Loss (Psychology) 4. Death--Psychological aspects.
5. Winter, Aurora--Diaries. 6. Widows--United States--
Diaries.   I. Title.

BF575.G7W56 2003   155.9'37
                         QBI02-201045

Aurora Winter

Dedicated to my teacher,
my student,
and the light of my life,
my son Yale.

Thank you for making
my heart sing.

Joy and Sorrow

Then a woman said, "Speak to us of Joy and Sorrow."
And he answered: Your joy is your sorrow unmasked.
And the selfsame well from which your laughter rises
was oftentimes filled with your tears.
And how else can it be?
The deeper that sorrow carves into your being,
the more joy you can contain.
Is not the cup that holds your wine
the very cup that was burned in the potter's oven?
And is not the lute that soothes your spirit,
the very wood that was hollowed with knives?
When you are joyous,
look deep into your heart and you shall find
it is only that which has given you sorrow
that is giving you joy.
When you are sorrowful, look again in your heart,
and you shall see that in truth you are weeping
for that which has been your delight.
Some of you say, "Joy is greater than sorrow,"
and others say, "Nay, sorrow is the greater."
But I say unto you, they are inseparable.

KAHLIL GIBRAN

Aurora Winter

For everyone who has ever had
a broken heart.

May you find comfort and hope,
insight and inspiration.

Aurora Winter

Struggling and Soaring with Angels

Healing a Broken Heart

Contents

Foreword: Seeding Hope

Hearts break every day, everywhere. Yet they can also heal. Tragedy pierces our attention like a wailing siren. Healing can slip by unnoticed, like the gradual opening of a rose. A broken heart can be such a public thing, like a soaring mountain erupting with lava and volcanic ash, visible for miles. Healing, its mirror image, can be such a private thing, like a lake, its secret depths and craggy contours hidden from view.

The danger in this is that broken hearts may despair of ever healing. And that is what motivated me to share my own intimate diary and write this book. I do not want my injured brothers and sisters to sink in the quicksand of depression. I want to walk along beside you with compassion, understanding, and love. Step by step. From grief to peace.

I have poured out my heart and soul to those who follow me down this arduous, yet transformative path. I pray to that which is infinite that this message of understanding, forgiveness, and joy be magnified and multiplied beyond what I can personally achieve.

The actions of one person, acting alone, can make a difference. The actions of many people, acting together, can change the world.

Make a difference by passing this book on to someone else after you have read it. Spread the word. Spread hope.

Love is action.

God bless you,

Aurora Winter

Aurora Winter

Introduction

This book is a map showing the way home. It's like a song of healing specifically attuned to a heart devastated by loss, struggling with change, or despairing that life has lost all joy.

For that is how my own heart felt.

I suffered excruciating torture in my own personal version of hell.

Then I languished, despondent and despairing, mired in purgatory.

Yet now, my life is richly blessed and filled with so many miracles that I'm in paradise.

How did that happen?

That's an inspiring story, and one I will reveal. But we need to start at the beginning. As you read, I invite you to be willing to perceive that things are not always as they first seem.

This is my story...

Struggling and Soaring with Angels

Aurora Winter

I. TRAGEDY

*Pummeled by a waterfall of grief so intense and powerful,
it takes all my strength and concentration
to simply remain standing under the assaulting deluge.
Or I surrender—and I'm swept away.*

Struggling and Soaring with Angels

Premonition

I dream that I'm walking toward a door. An ordinary door in an ordinary room.

I open the door, continuing on my way. Immediately, I regret that innocent step, for the door opens into a black void.

There is no floor. No ceiling. No walls. Just emptiness stretching on forever and a wind that howls its loneliness and whips my hair into my stinging eyes.

Desperate, I try to scramble backward to safety, but it's too late.

Relentless, gravity claims me. I plummet into dark emptiness.

&

The only thing that makes life possible is permanent, intolerable uncertainty; not knowing what comes next.

URSULA K. LEGUIN

Aurora Winter

Tragedy

The nurse plagues me with questions. "What's his name? Where do you live?"

I want to scream at her, *Don't you know my husband's not breathing? I don't belong here! I belong at my husband's side!*

I race toward Emergency, toward closed doors. The fireman who administered CPR in the ambulance exits. He sees the question on my face. "I'm sorry."

And then I know he's dead. My husband is dead.

The fireman envelops me, comforts me with a hug. I feel heat and sweat and caring. He tried so hard to revive him. And failed.

Everything is a blur. The air is thick like water. Everything is muffled. Everything is in slow motion.

David lies on a hospital bed in a room alone. He could be sleeping. His body is still warm.

I bawl and wail my grief, words tumbling out, a torrent of things I need to say. I nestle my head against his chest, like I did when we were sleeping. I feel soothed, I feel heard.

He is still here. He is lingering in the air, lingering in the warmth of his body.

I pour my heart out to him, I tell him how much I love him. Hours later, I grow quiet. Finally, I lift my head from his chest, where it had lain safe and sheltered in love every night for ten years.

Gradually, family members arrive. Everyone has the opportunity to say good-bye. Everyone except our four-year-old son.

Struggling and Soaring with Angels

&

I have been driven many times to my knees
by the overwhelming conviction
that I had nowhere else to go. My own wisdom
and that of all about me seemed insufficient for the day.

ABRAHAM LINCOLN

Aurora Winter

The Promise

He died at 4 a.m., and it is afternoon before my family pries me from his side.

We all need some rest, some quiet time, some tea. I don't want to leave him all alone. But they insist. Reluctantly, I let them tear me from his side, promising my husband that I'll return.

Hours later, I'm no longer eager to race back to my lover's side—but I refuse to break my promise. My family tries to dissuade me. But I won't listen to reason. I don't comprehend reason. I am adamant. I *promised.*

Ignoring their entreaties and my own growing sense of dread, I return to the hospital. But my husband is no longer in the room where we'd left him. He is in the morgue. *How could they?!*

A long walk down a corridor. Footsteps echo hollowly. Only my promise keeps me putting one reluctant foot in front of the other.

With an overwhelming sense of dread, I see the sign on the door: The Morgue. I force myself to enter. A body lies on a cold, gray, steel slab. The searing image of death burns into my eyes, assaulting me. Screaming at me.

He doesn't look asleep any more. He looks violated. He looks dead.

But I kept my promise.

Struggling and Soaring with Angels

&

Either do not attempt at all,
or go through with it.

OVID

Aurora Winter

Telling Our Son

God loves little children. Our four-year-old didn't see his father die. Didn't get caught up in the flurry of firemen and paramedics. Didn't hear my anguished cries. Didn't see the ambulance take his father away at four a.m. All that is a blessing.

But how can I tell him that his father isn't coming home again? How can I tell him that his father is...dead? I am so tired. This day has seen so much already. Surely I've endured enough for one day.

But this isn't the kind of thing to postpone. Everyone's weeping and moaning. I have to tell Yale.

I sweep him into my arms. I explain things as simply as I can. I tell him his father had a big Owie. He went to the hospital, but the doctors couldn't make him better. Daddy wouldn't be coming home again.

Yale slides off my lap, pushes this away, and I let him go. He blots out this truth, losing himself in his video games. It's too much for him to absorb.

That's not surprising. It's too much for me to absorb. Dead? I just can't say "dead." It's so...final.

Every few hours, Yale emerges from the preferable world of video games. He asks me again and again, ever-hopeful, with innocent, trusting faith, as if he simply didn't hear me the previous times, "Daddy's in the hospital?"

"Yes," I reply. "Daddy's body is in the hospital."

He confidently assures me, "The doctors will make Daddy better. The doctors will fix Daddy's heart."

I yearn for that to be so. I yearn to tell him that the doctors are making Daddy better, that he'll be back home in

Struggling and Soaring with Angels

a few days, or maybe a week. But I tell him the truth. His little face twists into a dark knot. He rebels against this unspeakable betrayal, leaving me abruptly.

At the end of this longest day of my life, drained and soul-shattered, I tuck my beautiful son into bed with me, safely ensconced at a friend's house. My son pats my arm and reassures me. "The doctors will make Daddy better. The doctors will fix Daddy's heart."

I look into his hopeful, trusting eyes, and it kills me to crush the light within. I can't do this. Not again. Lord, haven't I suffered enough already? You've ripped out my heart—how can you make me rip out my son's heart? I hesitate. Would it be so terrible to let him fall asleep with hope, comforted by a lie?

"When is Daddy coming home?" my four-year-old asks, his eyes shining with such innocence it makes my heart ache.

I will not add to his heartache by breaking his absolute faith in me. I refuse to betray his trust with a lie. Let something of value survive this day unbroken! Somehow, I find renewed strength. As gently as I can, I repeat the mantra, "Daddy's not coming home."

Not ever again.

&

You must do the thing you think you cannot do.

ELEANOR ROOSEVELT

Aurora Winter

10

Ghostly Image

In the morning, my girlfriend tells me that she saw David walking up the stairs to our bedroom. She saw him very clearly, even saw what he was wearing (his sailing shorts, his yachting shoes). Did he come to the bedroom to bring me strength?

&

*What the caterpillar calls the end
of the world, the master calls a butterfly.*

RICHARD BACH

Struggling and Soaring with Angels

Itchy Woolen Sweater

I sit in a room alone, withdrawn from the bustle of well-wishers, the grieving of family.

No words can comfort me. No touch can ease this pain. No thing can bring me joy.

I have the clearest sense that my body is an itchy woolen sweater. I just have to shrug, and it would fall away from me. I'd set my soul free. I could be with my beloved.

We used to lie in bed and cuddle, and joke that we were two souls entwined in heaven. When it was time to be born, God had to shake them to separate them (like gauzy twin-ply tissues).

The first soul was his, the second soul was mine. God told me I'd have to wait a bit, but assured me we'd be rejoined...we were soul-mates. Soul-mates in heaven. Soul-mates on earth.

My body chafes at me. I feel imprisoned in it. I wouldn't even have to *do* anything. Just shrug it off, and it would lie discarded at my feet, like a hideous woolen sweater knitted by some misguided aunt.

Then, I would float blissfully free. We would be reunited. Bliss.

My mind is intrigued by this possibility. Could it be that easy? I'm about to try it.

But then I remember...*Yale*. Like a whisper from another, *What about Yale?*

I won't leave our son an orphan. No easy way out for me.

Aurora Winter

12

&

'Tis more brave to live than to die.

MEREDITH

Struggling and Soaring with Angels

Half a Soul

I beseech you,
Don't leave me.
Not yet.
I have only half a soul.

I beg you,
Lay your soul
On mine.

Stay with me a while.
Give me strength
To bear
The unbearable.

&

*Your pain is the breaking of the shell that encloses
your understanding. Even as the stone of the fruit must break,
that its heart may stand in the sun, so you must know pain.*

KAHLIL GIBRAN

Aurora Winter

Facing Death

I'm afraid to return to the house where he died. I've sent others to look for my eternity band, a ring he designed for me: twin bands of gold, inset with tiny diamonds, intertwined just as our lives were, interlaced just as our fingers were, intermingled just as our souls were.

And they've returned empty-handed. The place on my finger where it belongs feels so naked. Just as the place at my side where he belongs feels so empty.

My most sensible feet-on-the-ground friend, Deborah, accompanies me. I tell myself, *There's nothing to be afraid of.*

It's not David's ghost I fear. He loved me. He wouldn't hurt me. It's Death.

Concealed below the surface of everyday life, just as a crocodile is concealed under the water, Death lunged with blinding speed, seized its innocent victim, and swallowed him whole. Death lingers here.

My nerves jangle as I enter our bedroom, the room where he died. It's empty except for a mattress on the floor. I breathe a sigh of relief. I go into the master bathroom and tear it apart, searching in every drawer and every box. But my ring's not here.

Not only has he left me, he's stopped loving me. The missing ring makes that clear. I feel so wretched and bereft.

We had just moved in the night before he died. It was our first night sleeping here, on a mattress on the floor. There are no fond memories here, no years of comforting *ahh...home!* energy. Just boxes, moving, unpacking, then...inexplicably, death.

Struggling and Soaring with Angels

15

Actually, that's not true. Even in one day, we made some good memories.

My desk broke under the strain of moving. David went to the hardware store, purchased an iron bracket, and immediately fixed my desk. He placed it in my office so that I would be able to write the next day. That was a sweet, loving thing to do. And quite unusual for him not to put it off, as our house was full of boxes, friends, and family.

And even though he was tired from a long day, my husband played video games with our son. He took his time reading him a bedtime story, then lovingly tucked him in.

When my husband finally called it a day, he went to soak in the bath, but we ran out of hot water. I boiled pots and sloshed water on the stairs, bringing steaming water to him in the tub. He grinned up at me and sank into his well-deserved bath. I felt warm and happy. So the last thing I did for him was a loving thing. Then we went to bed and fell into an exhausted sleep...from which he never awoke.

I look one more time for my ring...and I find it. It's just where I told my friends to look, where I myself looked just a moment ago. It's in my jewelry box in plain view.

I greedily clasp it to my breast, then put my eternity band on. I'm flooded with relief, reassured that my husband loves me. He's not angry with me, or, if he was, now he's forgiven me. In my heart, I know he put my ring back here. He has reaffirmed our love, our intertwined connection.

Aurora Winter

16

&

*There shall be eternal summer
in the grateful heart.*

CELIA THAXTER

Struggling and Soaring with Angels

The Funeral Home

Family escort me to the funeral home. Their arms are gently offered for support, but it feels as though they're shoving me toward doom.

So many decisions—burial or cremation? Which casket? Which urn? Every decision seems impossible. Everything feels wrong. I want to scramble backward, not go forward.

I balk, refuse this hurdle. I will not. I cannot. But the hurdle flows under my planted feet like water.

I cannot freeze time. And who would want to freeze time here, anyway, in this agony?

Cremation. That casket. That urn.

&

All the hardships that come to you in life,
all the tribulations and nightmares,
all the things you see as punishments from God,
are in reality like gifts. They are an opportunity to grow,
which is the sole purpose of life.

ELIZABETH KUBLER-ROSS

Aurora Winter

No Regrets

My anchor,
my strength,
my best friend,
my love,
my joy,
and now my sorrow:

Together we climbed
many mountains
and together we sailed
many ships.

A new adventure
always beckoned on
the horizon, and you
were my bold, fearless
captain at the helm.

Thank you for loving
me so truly and loving
Yale so freely.

I know in our time
together we shared
more love and more
joy than many people
experience in a lifetime.

So hold my hand, my love,
and help me say, "no regrets."

Struggling and Soaring with Angels

&

Do not stand at my grave and weep. I am
not there. I do not sleep. I am
a thousand winds that blow. I am
the diamond glints on snow. I am
the sunlight on ripened grain. I am
the gentle autumn rain....
Do not stand at my grave and cry. I am
not there. I did not die.

ANONYMOUS

Aurora Winter

The Funeral Service

The church is full. I sit in the front row, an arm wrapped protectively around our four-year-old son. There's a smiling photo of my husband, young, handsome, vibrant, full of life. The church is full because he was well loved, and because his death is so shocking, so unexpected. He was only thirty-three.

People get up to pay tribute. I do not speak, but my words are heard. My mother reads my poem, "No regrets." Another reads a poem I chose, "Joy and Sorrow" by Kahlil Gibran. The choir sings, "He's Got the Whole World in His Hands," a song I chose to reassure our son.

I do not cry. Safely wrapped in my arms, neither does my son.

After the service, I see the sea of faces, pale and shell-shocked, some contorted with emotion, others stained with tears.

They see their own mortality. They see their loved ones snatched from them. They see Tragedy. They see Death.

A line forms to comfort me. I hear whispers, "She's so calm."

"She didn't even cry!"

Roles are reversed. I am the one comforting. They're traumatized by the sudden shock.

They don't realize these past three days have been three years for me.

Struggling and Soaring with Angels

&

For death is the destiny of every man;
the living should take this to heart.

Aurora Winter

Wreckage

I feel violated. People crowd around the wreckage of my life. They watch my guts spilling on the floor, see my heart pumping geysers. It's as fascinating as a car accident.

No, worse. They're drawn like flies to an open wound. I don't want to give them the blood they crave. I want to shut them out, be impenetrable, form a hard scab. But I can't seem to stop bleeding.

I feel raped. Everyone knows everything about me. They're rummaging around, poking and prodding. Exposing my most private places: my most intimate feelings, my most cherished dreams, my most tender hopes. My heart lies mangled, bloody and naked in the harsh examiner's light.

I wish everyone would just go away and leave me alone. But I'm so frightened of being alone.

&

Then Job replied, "If only my anguish could be weighed
and all my misery be placed on the scales!
It would surely outweigh the sands of the seas"

JOB 6:1-3

Struggling and Soaring with Angels

Scattered Thoughts

Every day seems like so many days, I can't believe it. It seems like months have passed.

Grief is like a very bad cold—all in the throat and head and sinuses. As the head and heart are so divided, the blockage forms in the throat. The head insists that David is dead, and the heart screams with denial. The throat is choked, thick with this conflict.

Other people's feelings hit me physically. I have no boundaries. It's as if I'm a boat on the ocean. Their feelings wash over me, rock me like waves. I could capsize. I feel the connectedness of all things and all people. Other people's grief or anger washes over me, invading my space. I am no longer separate, no longer protected by my own cocoon.

My emotions frighten me. The strength of them. The tiny trigger required to release them.

&

*If there is meaning in life at all,
then there must be a meaning in suffering.*

VICTOR FRANKL

Aurora Winter

Inside Out

My clothes feel wrong. Not me. Some, like this silk blouse, are too smooth and sophisticated. Others, like my old jeans, hang off my body, and bring no ease, no familiar sense of comfort. My clothes feel as though they belong to someone else. I've lost my sense of self.

I've also lost my sense of self-consciousness. Emotions and being true to them are all that matters. I'm stripped of pride, except for a fierce pride in the honesty of my emotions. I hold my head up as I cry. I make no attempt to muffle my sobs or conceal my pain. I couldn't hide it anyway.

I want to scream. Scream at everyone to get out of my house, get out of my life, get out of my most intimate feelings. Yet I am terrified of being alone.

I've become an "inside-out" person. Everything that's private and intimate, everything that's normally hidden inside, is on the outside, exposed.

&

The worst loneliness is not to be comfortable with yourself.

MARK TWAIN

Struggling and Soaring with Angels

Enraged

Blazing with rage. Irate at being abandoned. Seething at having fear again, the fear of a vulnerable woman living alone. Are the doors locked?

Furious that I have to do everything by myself. Raise our son by myself. Incensed that I can't write day and night without sleep or food or interruption. Resentful that I can't go to sleep forever. Angry when I'm alone. Annoyed when I'm *not* left alone. Hemorrhaging with toxic emotion.

I take a pillow and slam it against the wall again and again. That feels good. But there's still so much poison trapped inside me.

How can I excise this wrath? What if I had a hysterectomy and cut out my womanhood? Would that do it?

My sweet albatross sleeps beside me. Thank God I'm not pregnant. Only pregnant with rage.

&

These are the times that try men's souls.

THOMAS PAINE

Aurora Winter

Expectations

Everyone wants me to be something. The grieving widow. The bitch. The goddess. The pure embodiment of love and truth. The prolific writer. The supportive daughter. The good mother.

I'm just me. I'm not perfect. Just a human being. With feelings. Pain. Hurt. Sorrow.

Don't abandon me for not living up to your expectations. I need you. I try to need no one...but I can't.

Maybe later. Maybe never.

&

Love each other or perish.

W. H. AUDEN

Struggling and Soaring with Angels

A Miracle

God is so efficient. When we looked for a townhouse to rent in North Vancouver, we circled several classified ads, but only one jumped out. *That's it. That's the one.* We went to see it and rented it immediately. It was perfect.

But not for the reasons we thought. We didn't know that an intern lived across the walkway, though it was his door I pounded on at 4 a.m., yelling, "Somebody help me! My husband's not breathing!"

We didn't (at first) realize that our good friends lived around the corner, good friends who sheltered Yale from the storm surrounding his father's death.

We didn't know the miracle that Yale had a friend who had also recently moved to this complex, a little boy he'd already come to know in a daycare seventy-five miles from here. A little boy the same age as my son who became his best friend, his lifeline, his savior. A little boy who made the unworkable workable, the abnormal normal, the unbearable bearable. A little boy whose father had also died.

What are the chances of that? God exists, and he loves little children.

&

Your mind cannot possibly understand God.
Your heart already knows.

EMMANUEL

Aurora Winter

Loneliness

Sometimes I tell myself I'm less lonely now than when David was alive. Before, if he was gone for a few days, I yearned for his presence so keenly. He used to tease me that I'd pout and get frosty in anticipation of his withdrawal and absence.

There are two options. One: David's soul really is within me, filling some of that void. Two: I'm in denial. Major denial. Colossal denial.

So much pain. My eyes are dull, sockets black, face puffy and tear-stained. These stupid scrawls cannot release my pain.

I'm gaunt. Haggard. But my belly swells with emotion, pregnant with pain. Let me birth it, be released from this bloating weight.

It would be a bloody birth. Matted hair clotted blood— a gruesome offspring. What is being born here?

&

Pain is God's megaphone to a deaf world.

C. S. LEWIS

Struggling and Soaring with Angels

Tidal Wave

A tidal wave hits me.
I shimmer,
become translucent.

Everything welcomed in.
Everything passes through.

To contain the tiniest emotion,
a tiny seed of emotion
would allow the wave to
catch me and crush me.

Smash me with the force
of a tidal wave
against concrete.

&

*Such is the irresistible nature of truth that all it asks,
and all it wants, is the liberty of appearing.*

THOMAS PAINE

Aurora Winter

30

Our Son's Nightmare

Yale whimpers and moans in his sleep. I comfort him, and he falls back asleep without waking. But then he awakes at 2:30 a.m., drenched in sweat, consumed by terror.

"My thumb, my thumb!" he wails, choking on his sobs.

"Did you have a bad dream about your thumb?" I try to soothe him.

He's frantic. "No! You know."

"Did you hurt your thumb?"

"No! You *know!*" Still caught in the nightmare, he's terrified. He thinks his thumb is gone.

I show them both to him (and all his fingers). He is washed with immense relief.

His thumbs are intact, but his family isn't. A family without a father is like a hand without a thumb.

&

Grandma said, "Into each life some rain must fall."
This should take care of us for life.

BIL KEANE

Struggling and Soaring with Angels

Our Son

I grieve. I mourn. I weep.

Yet I am so angry! That you could betray me, deny me, abandon me, I can accept meekly. Maybe I deserve it.

But how could you leave your *son*? How could you?

My son has no father now. His thumb has been cut off. I lash out in fury, in impotent rage. I won't accept this meekly. He is *innocent*.

You'll never see his fifth birthday. Never see so many future things I'm not strong enough to think about. Our son. Our precious son.

&

If I can stop one heart from breaking,
I shall not live in vain;
If I can ease one life the aching,
Or cool one pain …
I shall not live in vain.

EMILY DICKINSON

Aurora Winter

32

Love – Hate

We had so much love. We lived love. Yin and yang. You die, and I discover my rage. So hard to be so furious with you, my sweet. Gentle words of love oft passed through these lips, but seldom words of anger. I choke on them.

But dare not deny any emotion. I pay tribute, I honor my love for you, the depths of my feelings, by expressing my true emotions.

I hate you for leaving me. I hate you for leaving our son. I hate you for hurting me so deeply.

But I don't regret this anguish, if that is the price of our love.

&

Truly, it is in the darkness that one finds the light,
so when we are in sorrow,
then this light is nearest of all to us.

MEISTER ECKHART

Struggling and Soaring with Angels

Rape

Brutal
relentless,
crushing,
he thrusts himself
upon her
against her will.

Terrified,
pleading,
beseeching,
entreaties—
all to no avail.

She was raped
in her own bed
in her own home.

Then, naked and bleeding,
dazed and disoriented,
she stumbles out into the world.

Men give comforting hugs
and she flinches, afraid.
Cruel women gossip,
said she asked for it,
and thereby violate her again.

Aurora Winter

Others stay away.
She's contaminated.
She's contagious.
She's out of control.

Protection stolen from her.
Privacy ripped from her.
Vitality stripped from her.

No mortal raped her.
Fate did.
A widow—
at thirty-one.

&

*The heart that breaks open
can contain the whole universe.*

JOANNA MACY

Struggling and Soaring with Angels

The Wall

There's a wall I cannot pass through. Each time I come to it, I veer away and fill the time with people and frantic activity.

The wall is loneliness. Profound loneliness.

&

Friends, I pray tonight,
Keep not your kisses for my dead, cold brow.
The way is lonely; let me feel them now.

ARABELLA EUGENIA SMITH

Aurora Winter

Drained

So drained.
I breathe in thin,
polluted air and
exhale blood.

I can't go on
like this.
I can't.

Too tired
to ask for help.
Besides—
who can bleed for me?

&

Surely, O God, you have worn me out;
you have devastated my entire household.

JOB 16:7

Struggling and Soaring with Angels

Something Inside Me Is Dead

Something inside me is dead.
Is it dead like a black rock,
glistening, beautiful and cold?

Or is it dead like spoilt meat,
a gangrene that will spread inside me,
poisoning everything?

&

We cannot let our angels go.
We do not see that they only go out
that archangels may come in.

RALPH WALDO EMERSON

Aurora Winter

A Four-year-old Fears Death

Yale asks, "Will I be dead when I turn five?"
I reassure him, "No, of course not."
But he frets, "If I exercise and eat good food, I'll live longer and longer?"
I agree, but he craves an absolute assurance I can't give. How can I promise him many years to live?
Youth promises immunity from Death, but it's like a lover's intoxicating promise, whispered in the night, evaporated in the morning. There's no guarantee. Death could claim him in a decade—or a dozen—or a day.

&

How do I love thee? Let me count the ways.
I love thee to the depth and breadth and height
my soul can reach....I love thee with the breath,
smiles, tears of all my life! And, if God choose,
I shall love thee better after death.

ELIZABETH BARRETT BROWNING

Struggling and Soaring with Angels

His Photograph

Today, I went shopping for Yale's first birthday without his father. I bought presents and groceries and picked up some photos I'd had developed.

Driving home, my curiosity gets the better of me. I can't resist sneaking a peek at the photographs. There's a close-up of my husband holding our son on his shoulders, ocean and mountains in the background. David's robin's-egg-blue eyes twinkle happily. Yale clowns around, secure in his father's strong grip. How could this photo have been taken just a moment ago? Already, it seems a lifetime ago.

Overcome by grief, I sob so hard I can't see to drive. I pull onto a side street and try to regain my composure. Still sobbing, I get out of the car and walk around. Fortunately, I don't wander too far as I lack the presence of mind to remove the keys from the ignition.

I can't regain my composure. Finally, still sobbing, I call my brother-in-law, Gerard, and he comes to my rescue. He meets me at Lonsdale Quay, and his simple presence consoles me. We walk along the shore, then sit in the park and talk about David.

And I had had the ridiculous thought that I'd be happy on such a sunny day, shopping for gifts for my son. Yale has been up three nights in a row and I'm exhausted. Tonight I'll sleep in the spare room, and my Mom will sleep with Yale.

I smell birthday cake. Tomorrow, we celebrate Yale's fifth birthday. Without David.

Aurora Winter

&

Even in laughter the heart may ache,
and joy may end in grief.

PROVERBS 14:13

Struggling and Soaring with Angels

Yale's Fifth Birthday Party

Balloons. Birthday presents. Wine glasses clink. Laughter rings out. The house is crowded with friendly people. Crackers and cheese are consumed along with sympathetic conversation.

I don't taste the wine. I'm not satiated by the food. I don't hear the conversation. I'm overpowered by loneliness.

His absence resonates through everything. I can taste it, touch it, hear it. Loneliness in a friendly crowd is so bitter.

I'm forced to realize that more people won't take away this loneliness or ease this pain. I'm silent. But inside, it is one long drawn-out scream.

&

Reality, looked at steadily, is unbearable.

C. S. LEWIS

Aurora Winter

Faith

I am not alone. What could be more horrible than this?
I am falling...falling...falling
...yet I am being gently caught.
I am not alone. That was an illusion.
Faith is born.

&

The Lord is my shepherd, I shall not want....
Even though I walk through the valley of the shadow of death,
I will fear no evil, for you are with me.

PSALM 23

Struggling and Soaring with Angels

Aurora Winter

44

II. TRANSFORMATION

Swimming in grief—no longer pounded
by a powerful waterfall of emotions—
but out of my element, no ground beneath my feet.
I've been through an earthquake
and I don't trust simple things—like ground— any more.
Sometimes, I find it hard to simply breathe.

Struggling and Soaring with Angels

Transformation

A nymph
steps out of a mountain pond.
Rivulets of icy water
run down her naked body.
Like tears.

She doesn't dry herself.
The wind slaps hair into her eyes.
She doesn't cry.
Her face remains immobile—
chiseled, angular.

Shadows shift,
perceptions shift,
as she buckles on black leather armor.
Steel studs gleam coldly.
Solemnly, she tightens each strap.

Steel whispers a lethal threat
as she draws her sword,
hefts its reassuring, dead weight,
then sheaths it.
Her eyes alone smile.

She walks away from the icy pool.
Her well-muscled black stallion
lies where he fell mid-stride.
His coat gleams with health
and a light sweat, but he is not lathered.

He is unblemished,
yet his eyes bulge—

Aurora Winter

open, glazed, unfocused.
He is undeniably—but strangely—dead.

She caresses his mane
which is groomed and
free of burrs.
Ignoring the jeweled bridle
and hand-wrought saddle,
she reaches into the saddlebag.
With savage gentleness,
she cradles a mewling babe.

Marble face impassive,
she looks down at the peaceful, green valley.
Heather and crocuses bloom.
Children play by neat houses
surrounded by the white lace
of fences and sheep.
She clenches her jaw.

Determined, she turns away
and strides up the steep, rocky mountain,
her destination shrouded in mist.
In her black armor, the Amazon warrior
looks fierce and formidable.
Except that, as she walks away, she leaves
traces of blood on the ice.

For her feet are bare.

&

A wounded deer leaps the highest.

EMILY DICKENSON

Struggling and Soaring with Angels

47

New Emotions

New emotions I discover—so vile, so ugly. Demons clawing out through my flesh. They will not be denied or sugar-coated.

Like hate. Unfamiliar feeling.

I hate being so impotent. Hate people treating me like a leper; seeing not me, but Death. Hate this gaping, raw black hole within me.

Hate people expecting me to be nice, polite, reasonable.

Hate myself for being nice, polite, reasonable.

&

*It's up to each of us to get very still
and say, "This is who I am."
No one else defines your life.
Only you do.*

OPRAH WINFREY

Aurora Winter

Sweat

Coming home from the gym, I can't bear to be still. I want to run and run and run. I could run all day and never get far enough away.

My mental anguish far exceeds my physical strength. I've already sweated for hours: biked and swum and rowed and lifted weights and run and sat in the hot tub and steam room and sauna.

It is not enough.

I spy my bike. I can go farther and faster by bike. I wheel it out onto the dark street, hopeful.

Under the stars I ride, pushing furiously, gasps so like sobs. I stand and push and push and sweat and sweat and sob and sob until exhausted (physically).

It is not enough.

&

I will tell you what I have learned myself.
For me, a long five or six mile walk helps.
And one must go alone and every day.

BRENDA UELAND

Struggling and Soaring with Angels

49

Defying Death

For the first time since our last sweet union, I feel like intense, passionate love-making.

A hot celebration of life. Sweat-soaked bodies, slippery, sticking, straining, throaty gasps, sweet ache, and ultimate shudders.

Celebrating life, worshipping life, *being* life. Prove that I am undeniably alive from lips to tongue to curling toes to deep within. Throw my vibrant aliveness in the face of Death—like a bucket of ice water—defiantly deny mortality.

The only problem is—the space in the bed beside me is empty.

Death cackles back at me, mocking this fool.

&

*It is only the bed that seems strange
and impossible to account for.*

RAYMOND CARVER

Aurora Winter

Single Mom

Single Mom. It seems so trite. My husband didn't just walk out the door. He's dead.

And I'm left to do everything "all by myself," as a child would say with pride. I want to prove I can do things "all by myself"—but this is ridiculous. I laugh. Always laugh when it hurts the most.

I'm tired of thinking about things, about others, about my career, I'm tired of planning tomorrow and the day after that and the irksome, tiresome day after that.

I want to be left completely alone in my misery and fill this book with my thoughts, then consume them for my sustenance.

&

Living is a form of not being sure,
not knowing what next or how...
We guess. We may be wrong,
but we take leap after leap in the dark.

AGNES DE MILLE

Struggling and Soaring with Angels

51

Irony

"My life is ruined," she wails.
Funny, he's the one who is dead.
"I can't go on," she moans, not thinking that he's the one
who cannot.
"I wish I were dead," she groans.
Be careful what you wish for—lest you get it, he warns.

&

Now and then, I go about pitying myself
and all the while my soul is being blown about
by great winds across the sky.

OJIBWAY NATIVE AMERICAN SAYING

Aurora Winter

52

Home Alone

The silence reverberates, filling everything.

&

Grief can take care of itself,
but to get the full value of a joy
you must have somebody to divide it with.

MARK TWAIN

Friendly Men

I'm surrounded by men who sincerely want to help me. What else do they want?

I'm suspicious of their motives, aghast at my own suspicions.

Married men. Friends-of-David men. Child-boy men.

How can I tell a friendly hug, a friendly kiss, from something more? I'm no good at this. I know that. Oscillating from too-suspicious to too-naïve and back again.

David, protect me from well-wishers, from my need for affection, from being misinterpreted—once again.

Tell them I'm married—isn't that true?

Or have these friendly men received some ghastly bit of news I've yet to comprehend?

Well, tell them I'm not available, not interested, not capable of loving some—mere shadow—of you.

&

Saying no can be the ultimate self-care.

CLAUDIA BLACK

Aurora Winter

No Words

I want to communicate with you so badly. But what do I want to say? I turn on the shower and undress, yearning to purify my muddy thoughts.

I'm hit by a rogue wave of anger. It's your son's fifth birthday and you're not here. You're not coming to any more birthdays, any more Christmases. You're not coming to his graduation, not coming to his wedding. You'll never see his wife, never hold his child.

Water rains on no one. I crumple to the carpet in a fetal position, sobbing inconsolably. But there are no words. Just the very loud sound of pure, wordless grief and agony.

ॐ

Weeping may linger for the night,
but joy comes with the morning.

PSALM 30

Struggling and Soaring with Angels

He Knew

His death was so sudden, so completely unexpected—or was it? Did he know, on some level, that he was leaving?

He did the things he would have done, had he known. He paid all the bills, tidied up his affairs. He had a will drafted. He made love to his wife the night before his last. And, most out-of-character—he cried.

He moved his family from a remote area to a safe place near friends and family the day before he died. He saw his family and many of his friends just hours before he died.

Although he was busy moving boxes into our new home, he took the time to walk each person to their car and thanked them for their help and said goodbye. His brother Gerard said that when he shook David's hand and said goodbye, the look deep into his eyes that David gave him troubled him for the rest of the day.

Perhaps, on some level, David knew he was saying goodbye—not just for a day—but for eternity.

&

No trumpets sound when the important decisions of our life are made. Destiny is made known silently.

AGNES DE MILLE

Aurora Winter

The Other Side

Black neck arched arrogantly, the loon bobs upon the glittering edge of perception. Without warning, it dives—and disappears. Expanding circles ripple, marking the hole it made when it left.

Wind-swept rollers surge in.

The loon is gone. Erased. The dark mirror gleams with tiny stars, impenetrable.

Wind-swept rollers surge in.

Nearby, the loon bursts out of the water, happily swallowing fish. It passed through some unknown dimension—and returned.

&

For what is it to die,
but to stand naked in the wind and to melt into the sun?
And what is it to cease breathing,
but to free the breath from its restless tides,
that it may rise and expand and seek God unencumbered?

KAHLIL GIBRAN

Struggling and Soaring with Angels

Memories

It seems so desperately important to remember all the details. Memories are all I have, and they slip away. Pictures fade to facts. Facts fade to generalizations. Can't I keep anything?

I crave David. Is my yearning holding him in some half-way place, keeping him from his destination? I must let go or my clutching may entangle him, like a fishing line might entangle that loon. If it can't dive into the depths, it won't be able to reappear—elsewhere—happily swallowing fish.

I've so often gazed deeply into his robin's-egg-blue eyes, so often had his head on my lap and stroked his curly auburn hair, so often caressed his ruddy, freckled face with my fingers.

Yet now I can't even conjure the image of his face into my mind's eye. It's as though he's been erased.

&

The field of consciousness is tiny.
It accepts only one problem at a time.

ANTOINE DE SAINT-EXUPÉRY

Aurora Winter

Curiosity

The range of my emotions astonishes me. For the first time, I feel *intrigued* to find out who I am all by myself, and see how this will turn out.

I've said before that I need only one person who loves me absolutely and I can do anything. Well, I'd better love myself absolutely.

&

Knowing others is wisdom.
Knowing yourself is Enlightenment.

LAO-TZU

Struggling and Soaring with Angels

Stranger

A strange face stares unblinkingly at me.

It is hauntingly familiar, yet unrecognizable. Ugly. A profound ugliness, deeper than the dark circles under the eyes, the puffy face, the dull eyes.

Someone I don't want to know.

The only problem is...I'm looking in the mirror.

&

The innocent mirror contains all, unashamed.
For this clarity, see yourself shamelessly. This is truth.
As a glass shines bright with polish,
so the heart's mirror will shine, the deeper you look.

RUMI

Aurora Winter

Walk Out the Door

If you wanted to leave me, why couldn't you just walk out the front door?

&

*The race is not to the swift
or the battle to the strong,
nor does food come to the wise
or wealth to the brilliant
or favor to the learned;
but time and chance happen to them all.*

ECCLESIASTES 9:11-12

Struggling and Soaring with Angels

Girl Talk

I sit, a bundle of tense energy, at a small table with a soul sister and two career women I have just met.

I order beer, change my mind, order a gin and tonic, change my mind, order a lime margarita. The waitress leaves. I wish I had ordered wine. Or soda water.

We chat. Fairly profoundly, considering. They are husbandless.

Twice divorced, Susan is now adored by a man she claims is her very best friend—yet she finds him wanting as a mate. I puzzle over that. Isn't a best friend a perfect mate? Laughing, she assures me he'll accompany her down the aisle, either as her fiancé—or as her maid of honor! How odd, I think. She searches for the perfect mate.

I had my perfect mate. And best friend, too.

Cheryl is forty, never married, confident. She's quit her job, dissatisfied, though unsure why. I urge her to follow her bliss, to read *The Heroine's Journey*. She searches for the perfect career.

I am following my bliss. I wish I was at home writing.

Susan details her prospects, listing their attributes: looks, money, house.

What about being best friends? Soul mates? I feel a surge of pity for these husbandless women—which turns to revulsion as I realize I, too, am husbandless.

The restaurant buzzes. I disconnect from the conversation about golf, thinking I can escape briefly by going to the washroom. Then I'll call David, touch base,

Aurora Winter

tell him the ladies' night is wearing thin, but I'll be home soon.

My wandering mind crashes back into the straight-backed chair as I remember I can't phone David. He's dead. I fight the urge to leap to the washroom to throw up. I force myself to remain seated.

The coffee and the bill can't come fast enough. I wish I could breathe.

&

Man loves little and often;
woman much and rarely.

ANONYMOUS

Struggling and Soaring with Angels

Love: Want or Need?

I wonder, as I drink tea at Lonsdale Quay, whether being loved and cherished is a human need—or a luxury? A luxury, I conclude, thinking of so many lonely souls.

But forget humanity. What about me? Need or luxury?

I'm terrified I'll accidentally fall in love. I know I'm a very "all or nothing" person. I cannot hold back, do things part way. I'm sure I would end up hurt, used, tarnished. I want David. Want his arms around me.

All or nothing. My temperament. My life. For I have gone from all…to nothing.

&

There is nothing so wretched or foolish
as to anticipate misfortunes.
What madness is it in expecting evil before it arrives?

SENECA

Aurora Winter

Botulism?

As we puzzle over what killed David, my father has an interesting theory: botulism. Perhaps in the Chinese food we ordered. Dad says that botulism toxin is extremely virulent, and it is not necessarily evenly distributed through the food. So if David's favorite dish, the lemon chicken, was contaminated, it could easily cause death. Hmmm.

For the last few days, my body has been very unhappy. I've been taking all sorts of multivitamins, but still seem to be getting sicker. Yale is sick, too.

&

To keep the body in good health is a duty...
Otherwise we shall not be able to keep
our mind strong and clear.

BUDDHA

Struggling and Soaring with Angels

Afraid

Tonight, for some reason, I'm afraid. Alone in this house with my son, I check that the doors are bolted, the glass patio door double-barred.

I hear creaking noises. Is someone in the house, or is the house just settling? Afraid to confront that fear, I face a more urgent one and check that my son is still breathing. He lies limp on the mattress where his father went peacefully to sleep one night and never awoke. My heart stops. But his warm breath on my fingers assures me that he's just sleeping. *Oh, thank God, thank God!*

I glance at the clock. Aghast, I see that it is precisely midnight.

My head suddenly grows a large, heavy headache. I curl up on the side of the bed where my love last lay, last breathed, and I guard my son's every breath like a dragon guarding her hoard.

I survey the blank walls, the cold hearth. I have a lot of work to do to make this house a home, this twosome a family. I am determined.

Aurora Winter

&

Use your imagination
not to scare yourself to death
but to inspire yourself to life.

ADELE BROOKMAN

Struggling and Soaring with Angels

His Trench Coat

I pull on David's trench coat. I feel his presence. I'm overcome with emotion.

It sweeps the floor. Deep auburn, like his curly hair. I think I'll keep it and wear it. Everything will be okay.

&

The mind that is anxious about the future is miserable.

SENECA

Aurora Winter

Going Down

I walk down the many stairs in my townhouse. Going down and down and down feels right.

But then, there are no more stairs. Miserable, I sit on the bottom step and sob.

&

The mind has a dumb sense of vast loss—that is all.
It will take mind and memory months and possibly years
to gather the details and thus learn
and know the whole extent of the loss.

MARK TWAIN

Struggling and Soaring with Angels

Eli's Lesson

The producer called to finalize the travel arrangements for my research trip to the Hutterite colony in Saskatchewan for this movie I'm writing. I'm having a hard time focusing on this script, *Eli's Lesson*. What is his lesson, anyway? I can't see the profound truth in this little adventure story. I want to make it better, make it more mine, but still keep within the producer's parameters. I'll do my best.

On another project, a TV series I co-created entitled *On the Brink*, Mel Tuck and I agree to continue working side-by-side and to share "written by" and "created by" credit equally. I feel blessed to have this revered director and acting teacher as my writing partner. It is amazing to have professional actors workshop the scenes we write. What a learning experience!

&

The high prize of life, the crowning fortune of man,
is to be born with a bias to some pursuit
which finds him in employment and in happiness.

RALPH WALDO EMERSON

Aurora Winter

We Don't See Daddy Very Much Any More

"We don't see Daddy very much any more," Yale observed.

Which was not that strange, because his father is dead.

"I'm thinking about Daddy. How great it would be if he was still alive. He would be good at 'Flying Mario' because he was better than me at plain 'Mario.'"

A little later, with the pragmatic unselfconsciousness of a five-year-old, he asks, "Are we going to get a new Daddy?"

I tell him that his Daddy will always be his Daddy, even though he is dead.

"I always love you, Mom, even if you're dead," Yale announces solemnly.

Tonight, he sleeps in his own bed for the first time since his father died. At least until he crawls into my bed at 3 a.m.

"I love you, Mom. I always love you. Even if you are dead, I love you."

I snuggle him. "I love you, too, Yale. I'll always love you. Even if I am dead, I'll still love you."

&

I'll love you forever. I'll like you for always.

ROBERT MUNCH

Struggling and Soaring with Angels

Overflowing with Love

This evening I feel full of love. I love David so much. This love spreads all over, now that it lacks his physical presence to focus on. I love so many people.

And you know? If you love people, they love you back. It's astonishing. And simple.

I guess everyone wants to be loved. Give a gift of love—and you'll likely get the same gift back.

&

The heart is like a garden.
It can grow...compassion or fear...
resentment or love....
What seeds will you plant there?

BUDDHA

Aurora Winter

Ghostly Kisses

Lying in bed (on the side of the mattress where David died, in the room where he died), I have the gentle impression I'm being kissed by some ghostly presence. My lips tingle ever so slightly. I feel I'm being hugged, some presence against my body.

&

Love your life. Accept the beauty offered you for what it is. Don't question it. Don't analyze it.

HENRY DAVID THOREAU

Struggling and Soaring with Angels

Incompetence

I'm crushed by a feeling of incompetence, of worthlessness. I wish I were dead! It's been almost two months. Years more of this to endure.

Why doesn't he come back from this extended business trip?! How can I care enough to keep going? Nobody really loves me. And why should they?

I'm still so vulnerable. Arrogance and conceit (to think that I can handle this) mixed with insignificance and incompetence. An unlovable mix.

To top it off, I hate myself for wallowing in self-pity.

&

We were born to make manifest the glory of God
that is within us. It's not just in some of us;
it's in everyone. And, as we let our own light shine,
we unconsciously give other people permission to do the same.

NELSON MANDELA

Aurora Winter

A Five-Year-Old on Love

"I love you more than Dad." Yale pauses, waiting for a reaction. Not getting one, he continues breathlessly, "I love you more than my new clothes or more than my video game or more than anything! I love you more than 'Flying Mario.' (That's a hard-to-believe-one, isn't it?) I love you more than going on an airplane. (Whoa!) I love you more than this new house that we're living in now." (A condo in Hawaii.) "I love you more than Santa Claus and more than presents. (Whoa! Isn't that good?!) I love you more than anything! I love you more than a star!"

"I love you more than that!" I protest. "I love you four million-billion-zillion. I love you like crazy wildfire. I have the galloping greedy gimmies of love for you! You are the light of my life, the joy of my joy, the happiness of my happiness!"

I tickle him, and he giggles happily, then asks, "Do you love me more than Dad?"

I pause, then gently say, "No."

"Why?"

"I love you both the same—four million-billion-zillion!"

"I love you with all my might. Say that on it, Mom."

I comply, writing it down.

"Read it to me."

I read it back to him.

"Write down, 'I love you' at the end of it," Yale says.

I do.

Yale says, "Love is an important thing. Write that down."

Struggling and Soaring with Angels

I do.

Yale says, "I love you more than outer space."

"I'll write that down."

"I'll remind you. Did you forget yet?" Yale teases.

"No, not yet," I say, writing it down.

"I thought of another one!" Yale crows excitedly. "I love you more than my new fishing rod. (That's hard to believe!) And I love you more than my bow and arrow!"

&

*All we need to make us really happy
is something to be enthusiastic about.*

CHARLES KINGSLEY

Aurora Winter

Dream: Swallowed Faerie

It's a Sunday night, the same night that he died. As with other Sunday nights, I sleep fitfully, troubled.

I dream that I am a tiny, ethereal faerie. She's just two inches high, but full of impish life and confidence, in spite of her tiny stature and fragile gossamer wings. She has magical powers, you see.

She's brought into a room to face an enormous, faceless man. The giant looms menacingly, crude and coarse and crass. But she's petulant, cheeky, unafraid.

After all, size doesn't matter when you have magical powers.

Behind her back, his enormous hand drops a dull silver necklace like a tiny chain-link fence over her head. He catches her by surprise. The necklace imprisons her, weighs her down, robs her of flight, nullifies her magic.

Sensing her doom, she whirls and faces the giant. Stripped of her magical powers, she's naked and vulnerable.

He laughs, evil on his mind, his erect penis loving her fear, craving her unspoiled purity, eager to defile her innocence. He forces her to have anal sex. It's a huge rape.

Too huge.

She falls into him, into the space between his cells.

He howls, thwarted, frustrated, and claws at his skin. But he can't reach her. She's trapped *inside* his body, in the empty space between his molecules.

She's escaped being raped, but this, in some ways, is worse. Violence exchanged for gray dreariness, and a life-time sentence.

Struggling and Soaring with Angels

Forever trapped in this loathsome body, fenced in by the tiny chain around her neck. A chain only her oppressor can remove—but he cannot. He can't reach her.

Doom.

&

*The Artist is a receptacle for emotions
that come from all over the place:
from the sky, from the earth,
from a scrap of paper, from a passing shape.*

PABLO PICASSO

Aurora Winter

Siesta

I take Yale for a walk, telling his Uncle Gerard and Aunt Melanie that we'll be gone at least 45 minutes— probably more. To let them know there's time for them to cuddle—or more.

On holidays, David and I used to make love every afternoon. I remember when we vacationed in Mazatlan, Mexico, we took a "siesta" every afternoon at about 1:30.

I remember lying by the pool together, reading the same page of the same volume of *Lord of the Rings.* That was so romantic, so wonderful.

&

*I understood how a man who has nothing left
in this world may still know bliss,
be it only for a brief moment,
in the contemplation of his beloved.*

VICTOR FRANKL

Struggling and Soaring with Angels

Tropical Downpour

This afternoon, the heavens open, releasing sheets of rain. I whip off my sundress and bolt outside in my bathing suit. There, I exalt in the warm downpour, galloping barefoot on the soft, wet grass beside the beach, like a filly made frolicsome by the wind.

Giddy with life, with the wonder of it all—rain, glorious rain! Completely uninhibited, swept up in the miracle of the monsoon, I dance my elation, my awe, my aliveness.

Old people peer out at me, safely sheltered from this joyous gift from God.

ᐧ᙮

Joy is prayer—Joy is strength—Joy is love—
Joy is a net of love by which you can catch souls.

MOTHER TERESA

Aurora Winter

Making Plans without Him

This morning, I went for an uninspired run. I kept getting weighed down with thoughts, and my jog would trickle off into a depressed walk. Then I would spur myself back into that plodding jog.

Later in the day, Melanie and Gerard and I talked about goals, and I spent the afternoon trying to visualize my future without David.

Everything seemed to trigger tears today. I wept about David, sad that he would never live in the house he designed and worked so hard to build. I wept because Melanie had dreamt of death the night David died, and I had had no sign. I wept because I felt betrayed by God.

Melanie and Gerard hugged me and reassured me. I don't mean to be such a burden. I just can't seem to stop crying.

&

Look not mournfully into the past, it comes not back again.
Wisely improve the present, it is thine.
Go forth to meet the shadowy future without fear
and with a manly heart.

HENRY WADSWORTH LONGFELLOW

Struggling and Soaring with Angels

Setting Goals

1. GOAL:

I have a beautiful home in Whistler (a ski resort in Canada) that my husband built, and that we visualized together. It is a place of love, harmony, and joy, and a place for personal and spiritual growth. I enjoy it with Yale and our extended family and friends.

Why this is a good goal:

It fulfils a plan that David and I made two years ago and honors David by achieving his dream. It minimizes regret and provides stability and continuity. Also, David predicted the house would appreciate substantially—we'll see if he's right.

It creates a home dedicated to my new extended family and reflects the new reality of "family" for Yale and me. Family and friends will join us in Whistler. The time spent together will deepen bonds of love and cement important relationships. Yale will feel more connected, more loved, and more stable.

Present Position:

I own a home in Whistler that is incomplete. Drywall is in.

Aurora Winter

Deadline:

David's birthday—June 28th. Host a party then, celebrating finishing the house that David built and celebrating David's life.

Obstacles:

Number of decisions required to complete the house and my difficulty making decisions—especially about the house. Money—cost of finishing the house, and extravagance of keeping it without David's income.

2. GOAL:

I am a successful writer. My work is produced. I am paid to write, and I support myself and my son with my income from writing.

Why this is a good goal:

In the words of Joseph Campbell, being a writer allows me to "follow my bliss." When I write, I feel true to myself, happy and fulfilled. This is the key to unlocking the rest of my life.

Present Position:

I am a fledgling writer. I have an agent. Several respected people in the film and television business believe in me.

I was paid to write my first script, *Dragon Claws*, and it won recognition, an award, and development financing, but was not produced. I am being paid to write *Eli's Lesson*. None of my scripts has yet been produced. It looks very hopeful that *Eli's Lesson* will be produced, and production is still a possibility for *Dragon Claws*.

Struggling and Soaring with Angels

83

The original TV series *On the Brink*, which I co-wrote and co-created with Mel Tuck has two one-hour scripts written, as well as a series bible. The whole package is currently in the hands of an L.A. agent.

Deadline:
    One year from now.

Obstacles:
    Pressure of dealing with other necessities and concerns due to David's death, and the resultant lack of a keel in my life. Feeling in a tailspin. Contacts required to obtain work. The fact that my scripts haven't yet been produced.

&

Do not manage as if you had ten thousand years before you.
Look you, death stands at your elbow;
make the most of your minute,
and be good for something while it is in your power.

CHARLES PALMER

Aurora Winter

Yale – Healing in Hawaii

After spending a week in Hawaii with his mother, Uncle Gerard, and Aunt Melanie, Yale looks much more like a normal five-year-old. His eyes are clear pools now. At the beginning of the week, they were knotted with anger and other troubled emotions.

His uncle is a lot like his father. Gerard's attention showered on Yale was very healing. I am grateful.

&

Listening is the oldest and
perhaps the most powerful tool of healing....
When we listen, we offer with our attention
an opportunity for wholeness.
Our listening creates sanctuary
for the homeless parts within the other person.

RACHEL NAOMI REMEN, M. D.

Struggling and Soaring with Angels

Letting Go of His Soul

A day I will never forget for the rest of my life. As I had done on so many other mornings, I rode my bike along a deserted gravel road through an ancient forest.

But this time wasn't like any other time, either before or since. This is what happened:

I thought I heard someone calling my name. Perplexed, I stop, scan the forest. I see only huge conifers standing like solemn guardians, hear only the chuckling of a brook. I shrug it off, and continue riding.

Then it comes again, *Aurora, Aurora, Aurora*. My heart catches. David's calling me. It's as clear as if he had spoken. I stop my bike again, barely daring to hope. "David?"

I search the forest. I see no one—only ancient logs crumbling into soil, the air so still not even the leaves tremble. Disturbed, I continue.

Aurora, Aurora, Aurora. His voice does not slip away as I ride. So his words aren't coming to me through the air. His voice isn't hurried or desperate or frightened, but insistent. He wants something from me. What?

I search the heavens. If the answer is hidden in the gray clouds covering the sky, it's too obscure for me to comprehend. I reach heavenward and call out, "I love you David!" I command my love, my life force, to flow from me to David. That seems good and right. But it doesn't feel like enough.

Aurora, Aurora, Aurora. David keeps calling my name. It's a plea, a request, a call for help. He's asking for something from me. What?

Aurora Winter

86

I search my heart. I realize how I would feel if we traded places. This is harder to say, harder to mean. I choke out, "I forgive you for dying, David." I break down and sob. Thunder claps.

Not satisfied, I gather my strength and say it again. This time my voice is strong and clear. I send my energy to him once again.

Aurora, Aurora, Aurora. Fainter now, thankful now, but there's still something missing. I want desperately to help him, if I can. He needs something from me. What?

I search my memory. I remembered the night after he died, I cried out that I only had half a soul and I begged him to lay his soul on mine and stay with me a while. I believe he did so.

Now, our souls are entwined together, his soul enmeshed with mine, and I'm holding on so fiercely he can't leave. But he needs to go. He doesn't want to, but he has to. And I have to let go.

The outside of my body is vibrating. Humming, kind of, but silent. I ride my bike to a friend's. I can't do this alone. It's too hard. My friend welcomes me into his home, ushers me into a quiet room. My body vibrates with increasing urgency. My skin tingles. Even the skin on my ears buzzes. How do you let go of someone's soul?

"You know what you have to do," my friend says.

I try half-heartedly to release this buzzing, vibrating energy, but nothing happens.

I don't really want to let go. The humming feeling becomes more and more pronounced. It feels like childbirth—an inevitable, painful process that is going to happen whether you help it out or not.

Struggling and Soaring with Angels

I gulp some water, steel my resolve, stand up, and focus my intent to release his soul. Nothing happens.

A soft suggestion comes out of nowhere. *Take your eternity band off.* I'm appalled. I can't do that!

You must. Enraged, I take off this most precious symbol of our love, of our future together, and fling it onto the floor.

I'm gently chided. *I don't want to leave like that.* I soften and drop my watch to the floor.

After a quiet moment, I tell David, "I love you. I forgive you. I release you." I stand up again, raise my hands to the heavens, and focus my clear intention to release him.

This time, I feel a surge of incredible energy gathering all over my body. Rising from my toes, it coalesces into a kind of lump, as if I had something in my body that's not mine. This energy surges, tingling, up through my body and out through my head.

And then the energy is gone. David's soul has gone.

I stumble to the washroom and throw up. Weak and spent, I shiver, ice cold. My friend swaddles me in blankets and gives me tea and toasted bagels.

I sit by the fire and see gray bubbles dancing around me in a strange double helix, like DNA. At this point, that doesn't even seem odd. My aura envelops me, comforts me, stays with me.

The most beautiful thing we can experience is the mysterious.

ALBERT EINSTEIN

Aurora Winter

Not Grounded

I feel insubstantial. The scale states 98.5 pounds. Impossible! I try again, expecting it to say approximately 115 pounds, but it insists: 98.5 pounds.

Did David's soul weigh so much? I feel shaky, as though I could float off into the next world easily. At the airport, a weight-activated door refuses to open for me.

I put a stone in my pocket. Leaning against a tree for comfort, I'm amazed to feel its life-force flooding me, replenishing my own.

What's happening to me? Some doorway has been opened. This is *not* normal.

∂

An abnormal reaction to an
abnormal situation is normal behavior.

VIKTOR FRANKL

Struggling and Soaring with Angels

Aurora Winter

III. Trials

꘡

*I'm walking in the rain. I'm relieved
to have land back under my feet,
in spite of the cold, stinging rain.
Sometimes, the clouds part,
and I find myself standing in a
warm beam of sunshine.
Ahhh—that feels good.*

Struggling and Soaring with Angels

Eli's Lesson

Sixty-six days ago, David died. Yet today I'm traveling to Saskatchewan to research a script that takes place on a Hutterite colony. Things set in motion prior to my husband's death continue to unfold, which somehow seems absurd.

I turn my attention to the gently rolling farm land. I reach the Arm River Hutterite colony: a simple church, a dozen homes, and several barns. Cousins to the Amish, Hutterites follow a strict Anabaptist religion.

Warm and welcoming, the Hutterites crowd around when I arrive. Most have seen little of the world outside the colony, so they're openly curious.

The minister, Dan Hoffer, gives me the grand tour of the farm: state-of-the-art milking parlor, automated chicken barn, meticulous machine shop. I see why the local farmers' respect for the Hutterites is tinged with envy.

Next, we tour the small village. In sharp contrast to their lavish investment in farm machinery, their lifestyle is as plain and frugal as their clothes. Like the Amish depicted in the movie *Witness*, the women wear long, dark dresses, the men wear sturdy, black work clothes.

Determined to immerse myself in their culture, I ask if I could dress as a Hutterite. The Hutterites smile approvingly, delighted by my request. One sincere young woman, "Sarah," leads me to her room and opens her closet. Taking off my filmmaker's "uniform" of black jeans and jacket, I slip into the dark frock that she gives me. It brushes my ankles. I feel that I'm going back in time.

Aurora Winter

Sarah helps me cover my short blonde hair with a kerchief. Satisfied, she observes, "You look like a proper Hutterite now."

Looking in the mirror, I'm amazed by the complete transformation. I feel deeply uneasy, as though my identity came off with my clothes. As if surrendering my clothes amounted to surrendering my passport. As if I could be absorbed, assimilated, and trapped here forever.

"Are you married?" Sarah asks.

"Yes. No. I mean, I was. But my husband died two months ago."

Sarah says, "God takes away whatever—or whoever—we love too much. To remind us to love Him before all else."

I try to dismiss that startling notion, yet I feel a sharp stab of fear. Would He take Yale next?

&

Truth is only relative and not absolute.
All truth is only so within a certain level of consciousness....
Perception is not reality.

DAVID HAWKINS, M.D., PH.D

Struggling and Soaring with Angels

Utopia?

Bells regulate my life. A bell to wake, a bell to worship, a bell to gather. In the dining room, men sit on one side, women on the other. Everyone sits in prescribed places, in order of their age.

A bell rings, and the minister says grace. Another bell, and people start eating. I try to engage in small-talk, but am shushed. This time is meant for eating, not "frivolous" conversation. After fifteen minutes, another bell rings. Everyone stops eating, and women efficiently clear the plates. Not accustomed to bolting my food, I've barely touched my meal. But I have more than enough food for thought.

The Hutterite colony operates like a big extended family. Everyone contributes according to their ability. Everyone is cared for. Widows don't struggle to survive. Neither do they scramble to find child care. All the children have many aunts and uncles looking over them. I begin to have a deeper appreciation for the Hutterites' version of Utopia.

At the one-room school house, Sarah explains that a teacher comes during the week, and teaches grades one through eight. I ask about higher education and career choices. Sarah laughs at my city notions. "Grade eight is plenty of education to milk a cow or plant the fields. We're all farmers—anything else we need to know, we can learn right here on the colony."

I'm taken aback, realizing this version of Utopia would not work for me.

Aurora Winter

Returning Home

Leaving the Hutterite colony and my new friends, I return home. Happily reunited with my son, I read him a bedtime story, then kiss him goodnight. Turning out the light, I feel thankful. He may not have a father, but he has so much. And so do I. We both have so many choices, so much freedom. I'm determined to be a warm wind under his wings, helping him soar, helping him follow his own dreams.

I feel compelled to deepen the script. I want something more profound than an adventure story about a Hutterite boy who runs away on Halloween. I'm driven by a need to touch someone's soul with a message that really matters.

I decide to give the young hero, Eli, a dream. An impossible dream that burns within him so fiercely that it drives him to leave the colony and everything safe and familiar. Hutterites are farmers whose fate is inextricably entwined with the soil. So I decide that that most unattainable dream for Eli is to yearn to be a pilot, flying free, flying high in the sky. I give Eli the hopeless dream of becoming a pilot.

As I struggle late into the night with plot and character and motivation, I reconnect with my own dream of being a writer; and that brings me, if not happiness, at least a glimmer of joy.

Struggling and Soaring with Angels

95

&

You are what your deep, driving desire is.
As your desire is, so is your will.
As your will is, so is your deed.
As your deed is, so is your destiny.

FROM THE BRIHADARANYKA UPANISHAD

Aurora Winter

When Will This End?

When will this *end?* I'm still in so much pain. I feel as though I'm walking around bleeding, gushing blood from my heart. I grow angry and impatient. I'm sick of being in pain!

I'm so fragile—I can't even prioritize my week (which has a few minor conflicts) without bursting into tears. I get a headache just making a "to do" list. If David were here, he'd cut through my haze of confusion. He always did.

He used to call me his pixie princess. I smile, thinking of that. But I don't feel like a pixie princess any more. I keep bursting into tears. I hurt. I hurt. I hurt!

Do people expect me to be better by now? I'm not.

But maybe the person who thought I would be better by now…is me.

❧

How poor are they that have not patience!
What wound did ever heal but by degree?

SHAKESPEARE

Struggling and Soaring with Angels

Dream: Season's Tickets

I'm in a stadium, buying season's tickets. I think it would be fun to look forward to an ongoing event with my son.

I'm wearing an expensive, serious suit. I'm carrying a lot of valuable stuff: briefcase, purse, cellular phone. I fret, burdened, and spend a lot of time trying to find a safe place to lock up my things. But there's no safe place. I can't put anything down.

The dream changes. A greaser talks to me. He's "white trash"—not the kind of person I'd normally associate with. I'm drawn to him because he talks about grief. He seems to understand. He has grief from Vietnam. But as he talks, he contradicts himself. Little slip-ups: the year changes, the number of people who died changes. I don't trust him.

I'm afraid to go to my Toyota Forerunner, afraid that he will follow me and get in my vehicle. I can't think how to prevent that from happening if he tries. I do not confront him. Instead, I wait and wait.

Finally, he seems to be gone, although I don't see him leave. I hurry to my 4x4, my echoing footsteps betraying my presence.

Afraid that he might be lurking in the shadows, I pick up my pace, fumble anxiously with my keys, wrench the door open, jump in, and lock the doors. I'm flooded with relief.

Now relatively safe, I drive away, down a winding, desolate road. I become convinced that he's following me. I'm afraid.

Aurora Winter

I encounter my Dad driving a tractor. For some reason, we change vehicles. The tractor seat slopes precariously, and I have the sensation that I'm going to fall over at any second.

My Dad goes on ahead. I feel vulnerable and exposed in the slow-moving, open, listing vehicle. I try to follow my Dad, but he drives into a space ship and it takes off into the night sky.

The wind howls. The tractor lists. I am exposed, abandoned, and now—falling.

&

Avoiding danger is no safer in the long run
than outright exposure.
The fearful are caught as often as the bold.

HELEN KELLER

Struggling and Soaring with Angels

Blood Money on Mother's Day

I have the life insurance money. I feel like throwing up. David really is dead. Hateful proof, horrid money. His life is priceless.

I go home, needing a nap. Some Mother's Day. But when I close my eyes, all I can see is David at the morgue. He looked definitely, irrefutably dead there. Irrefutably? Hah!

This understanding of "irrefutably" goes on and on. I get in a rage, cry angry tears, slam my pillow around. How can he be *dead?!*

How can I still keep a corner of denial? A dwindling corner.

&

Place me like a seal over your heart,
like a seal on your arm;
For love is as strong as death,
its jealousy unyielding as the grave. ...
If one were to give all the wealth of his house for love,
it would be utterly scorned.

SONG OF SONGS 8:6-7

Aurora Winter

Finishing the House

My brother Bryce and I drive to Whistler to see how the finishing is coming along. I can't believe the paint color is wrong again. It looked good on the paint chip, but terrible in the house. It's a murky, ominous purple, rather than a warm pussy-willow grey. Now the whole house needs to be repainted. Again. What a waste of money.

Every time I turn around, this house seems to be costing more money. Bryce reassured me that even professional interior designers often have to repaint—even several times. Next time, I'll paint a sample area. Bryce promised to help me pick another color, which is great. He's brilliant with colors.

My foreman had no idea how to put together the jigsaw puzzle of kitchen cabinets that David had purchased. It was a bit complex, but Bryce and I figured it out. David would be pleased.

Electricians and trades keep asking me where things are in the house or what David planned for this or that. I keep having to say, "I don't know." He had so many things in his head. I feel anxious about having to trust so many strangers. How do I know whether David had paid them or not? How do I know what agreements he made with them? I just have to trust that people won't take advantage of me.

I have so much anxiety about finishing the house. I don't feel I can trust myself to do it right. I've never built a house before. To be thrust into the process mid-stream like this—it's a recipe for disaster.

Struggling and Soaring with Angels

I don't want David to be disappointed with how it all turns out. He put so much of himself into this house.

&

What's terrible is to pretend
that the second-rate is first-rate.
To pretend that you don't
need love when you do;
or you like your work when you know
quite well you're capable of better.

DORIS LESSING

Fighting Depression

When David died, I felt as though I was walking through water. Even sound seemed muffled. I had to push through the weight of the water. It dragged against me. An incredible G-force weighed me down.

Now, I feel as though I have lead in my veins. The heaviness doesn't push down upon me from without, but from within.

Everyone wants a piece of me, it seems. There is only a trace of me here. And as pieces are taken (or given with love), there is only a ghostly scrap remaining. I must be careful.

My mom isn't doing very well since my father left her for another woman. Next week is my parents' wedding anniversary, and she feels so lonely without my father, so rejected. She's almost suicidal. I try to be supportive, but I'm exhausted.

Being a single, working mom is so much work. Add grief, an incomplete house in Whistler, a new career, a family in chaos of separation, and the result is overwhelming. At least, it hardly leaves time to feel lonely. I'm too exhausted and drained.

I have a tiredness, a listlessness that I can't seem to shake. Oh—to feel alive again. That would be pure joy. Patience, patience.

A horrible despondency creeps over me. A black cloud that makes everything dim and murky. Why bother? Who cares? Gone is that eagerness not to waste a precious,

Struggling and Soaring with Angels

bright day; not to waste a single moment. Wakefulness is dreary and dull.

Where is David's pixie princess? Where is "Aeroba," charged with energy, bopping around? Where is that determined, eager writer who never has enough time to set words to a page? Dreary, depressed Diedre is here, listless and dull and uninspired.

I lie in bed. I don't want to do anything with this afternoon. I just want it to be over. Just want to seek the oblivion of sleep again. Not a very positive attitude.

I decide to phone a therapist. I've never been to see one before, and it's $100 an hour. But I'm desperate. I hope she can help me find the key to myself. I hope she can help me lose "Diedre" before she settles in permanently.

&

*Concentrate your energy
and hoard your strength.*

SUN TZU

Aurora Winter

Heart Stone

I have a heart-shaped rock, a human heart, not some plastic valentine shape. Fist-sized and kidney-red like that organ. I found it in Saskatchewan, by the Arm River Hutterite colony on a dirt road on April 25th—one month ago exactly.

Once, when I lay in my backyard sunning, I held this rock in my right hand and dozed, only to be startled by the sensation of a gentle beating seemingly emanating from my heart stone.

A thin veneer of concrete coats one third of my heart stone. This scab clings with the tenacity of a barnacle. When I found my heart stone, I thought: when I work this scab free, my heart will be whole again.

I rub the rock, turn it in my hand, caress it with oil, bring it in the bath with me, warm it with candlelight (and even scorch it once). Usually, my efforts provoke no release. But every now and again, a flake of concrete suddenly pops off.

I'm glad, yet frightened. Hopeful, but afraid of being whole.

&

God doesn't require you to succeed;
He only requires that you try.

MOTHER TERESA

Struggling and Soaring with Angels

Yale Stone

I have another rock. It is smooth, alabaster-colored, with a coppery blush. The size of a small egg, and nearly the same shape, but flatter.

I cherish it because Yale gave it to me. He was watering Grandpa's raspberry bushes (a boy's bliss—a hose and dirt). Grandpa and I watched him from a distance, opening our hearts to each other.

"Mom! Mom! Look what I found! It's for you!" This stone clenched in his little fist, Yale ran eagerly uphill toward me, his face beaming.

I met him, and he gave me this gift, babbling happily about how he saw the white stone glinting like a star on the dirt, and that it was for me. He harvested this happy memory in the field where I gamboled as a child, where I galloped my mare, walked my 4-H steer, and had my first kiss.

I carry it in my pocket often. Every time I roll it in my hand, it makes me smile. The memory of Yale's infectious enthusiasm is embedded in this delightful stone.

&

Exuberance is beauty.

WILLIAM BLAKE

Aurora Winter

106

Bite by Bite

Another despondent day—ending ⸻
uplifting of my spirits. My father and I, bo⸻
both adrift, converse.

As the evening closes, I find I am cheered. Not superficially, for he did not try to cheer me with platitudes or solutions, but hope springing from deep within.

Hope stirred by his simple presence, by the stimulation of shared ideas, by talking about bliss. He suggested that I divide the dreary year of recovery I anticipate into thirds.

This simple suggestion cheers me profoundly. I'll conquer this imposing mountain by dividing it up and tackling it piece by piece.

Quarters, I think. The first quarter is past already—survival.

The second, I've just begun. I'll dedicate it to healing.

My ultimate goal at the end of this year is to be whole and balanced; to have accepted my new reality; no longer to feel overwhelmed and grief-stricken; to have, at least occasionally, a sense of joy.

&

Hope begins in the dark,
the stubborn hope that if you just show up
and try to do the right thing, the dawn will come.
You wait and watch and work: you don't give up.

ANNE LAMOTT

Struggling and Soaring with Angels

Sealed with Love

In bed, I read by candlelight. The candle drips. Hot wax falls upon the gold chain I wear every day, sealing the clasp shut with a hot, waxy kiss. The pendant is David's wedding ring.

Wax hangs in an unlikely rope an inch long, a perfect heart formed at its end.

The candle is scented. Sea mist. David loved the sea. And now he is mist. Is he reaching out to me?

&

If I die, take me to my lover,
There let me rest,
And should she kiss me once,
Don't be surprised if I live again.

RUMI

Aurora Winter

Depression

Sleep—the most blissful intoxicant left to me—beckons. I long to stay in that lover's grasp forever.

Wakefulness—a bloated, loathsome, leaden state abhorrent to my senses.

That tiresome state between sleeps.

Depression.

&

The mind has a dumb sense of vast loss—that is all.
It will take mind and memory months and possibly years
to gather the details and thus learn
and know the whole extent of the loss.

MARK TWAIN

Struggling and Soaring with Angels

Denial

I haven't seen David for more than three months. My daily conversation is liberally sprinkled with references to his death. Unskittish, straight-forward references: "Since David died," "I am a widow," "David is dead."

His clothes have mostly been given away or moved to another closet, except for those I wear and those precious few unwashed since he last wore them.

I've received the life insurance money. Enough time has passed that my answering machine lies quiet and unblinking for days on end.

I grieve. I have grieved. I mourn. I have mourned. I spill my feelings out, cry rivers of tears.

And yet. And yet...it still feels as though he might be away on some extended business trip. The truth slips away from me, ungraspable.

&

Truth, like surgery,
may hurt, but it cures.

HAN SUYIN

Aurora Winter

Shifted

Before, I was awkward with little children—uncertain animals with dirty paws.

Now, when I crouch and kiss my son goodbye, little children queue, wanting hugs, bestowing kisses.

It's not that they want to comfort me. Little children are healthily self-centered.

Rather, something inside me has changed. Now they are drawn to me.

&

I do believe it is possible to create,
even without ever writing a word
or painting a picture,
by simply molding one's inner life.
And that too is a deed.

ETTY HILLESUM

Struggling and Soaring with Angels

Make It *Stop*!

Every night, when I lay my head down on the pillow, it's with dread. Every night is the same. I awake in the middle of the night from the same nightmare. Reliving every second of his death.

I can't sleep. I'm so tired. I look haggard. My clothes hang off me. I try drinking before bed and fret that I'll become an alcoholic.

Deborah dismisses that worry, "Did you have a problem with drinking before?"

"Well, no."

"Don't worry about it. It's temporary," she says.

Still, a drink a night or even two is a lot for me, and an unfamiliar pattern. Besides, it doesn't work. I get homeopathic sleeping pills. But nothing takes a bite out of these nightmares.

His gasping breath. I turn on the light. His eyes are bulged, unseeing. "David, you're scaring me!" No response. I give CPR. He pees in the bed. Oh shit, oh shit, oh shit!

And I awake, drenched in sweat. I'm desperate. A friend recommends a therapist. I'll try anything.

"So, what seems to be the problem?" the therapist asks.

"I'm having nightmares. You have to make them stop."

"What are the nightmares?"

"They're nightmares of my husband dying beside me. He died a few months ago. I can't sleep. You have to make them stop."

"Well, just a minute here. Tell me more about your life," the therapist insists.

Aurora Winter

112

I don't want to get bogged down with details. I don't want to get all emotional and cry. I want *results*.

"How are you during the day?" the therapist prods.

"The days are okay. It's the nights that are a problem." *Make it stop, make it stop, you've got to make it stop!*

"How are you getting through the day?" the therapist persists.

"Okay. I just pretend that my husband is away on a business trip, and then I can function. It's the nightmares I can't bear." *Make it stop, make it stop, you've got to make it stop!*

"So—you get through the day by pretending that your husband is away on a business trip?"

"That's right." *It works. What's it to you?!*

"Maybe your nightmares aren't the problem," says the therapist.

What!? "What do you mean?"

"You're not living in reality. Your husband isn't away on a business trip. He's dead. Every night when you go to sleep, your subconscious reminds you of that fact. Over and over, like clothes spinning in a dryer, your subconscious mind is telling you the truth."

But I can't bear the truth!

"You have to deal with the truth. The dreams aren't the problem. They're the solution. Getting through the day by living a lie is the problem."

Oh.

Struggling and Soaring with Angels

&

In our sleep, pain which cannot forget
falls drop by drop upon the heart until,
in our own despair, against our will,
comes wisdom through the awful grace of God.

AESCHYLUS

Aurora Winter

Smug

"Wipe that smug smile off your face," said the Universe. For I was smug, having cleverly chosen to follow my heart when I fell in love with a gem of a man, a man who would never leave me.

I knew, if I fell ill, had a stroke, became a cripple, he would be steadfast.

I had been bedridden for languid months without medically-sanctioned cause, and he stood by me: patient, loving, giving.

I thought smugly, "I know what love is," and he had the same generous definition. I had found my soul-mate. I had reason to be smug.

But I had no right to be smug. I feared abandonment, and carefully arranged my life to preclude it. Yet...I have been abandoned. Tonight, that reality lacks the bitter sting it often has.

I'm not in control. Instead of thinking of my loss, I think of the gifts I have received, the love I have received—and given. David was a gift. Our love, our life together—a gift.

Tonight, in spite of everything, I believe that God loves me.

Struggling and Soaring with Angels

&

Gravy, these past ten years.
Alive, sober, working, loving and
being loved by a good woman.

Raymond Carver

Aurora Winter

Robert Bly

Dad reads to me from Robert Bly. "If you do nothing, I will do nothing. If you build a fire, I will chop wood. If you build a boat, I will be your ocean."

Profound. I will try not to let depression seize me again (and do nothing). I want to build, I want to sail the ocean. I'm determined. My life *will* have meaning.

&

There is a vitality, a life force, an energy, a quickening,
that is translated through you into action,
and because there is only one of you in all time,
this expression is unique. And if you block it,
it will never exist through any other medium
and it will be lost.

MARTHA GRAHAM

Struggling and Soaring with Angels

My Parents' Anniversary

My parents' anniversary. In spite of the pending divorce, Dad is taking Mom to dinner.

I hope they find the evening healing and not yet another emotional assault.

♄

We rejoice also in our sufferings,
because we know that suffering produces perseverance;
perseverance character; and character, hope.
And hope does not disappoint us, because God
has poured out his love into our hearts.

ROMANS 5 V 3-5

Aurora Winter

Inner Void

There's a void inside. In spite of my nausea, a queasy morning-sickness feeling, I try to fill the void with food.

A half-hearted attempt at self-abuse, perhaps, a vague reference to days long past when eating could soothe and comfort.

I don't even bother to throw up. I just feel worse—a bloated emptiness, laced with nausea.

&

Hot fudge fills deep needs.

SUSAN ISAACS

Struggling and Soaring with Angels

Chipped

We are born whole. Glittering. Golden. A perfect, luminous sphere. We roll carefree down the bumpy road of life and get chipped and cracked. If we lose too many fragments, we lose our clear vision of who we are. We lose our way.

I almost had the writer in me chipped away, a piece of me I didn't think I needed, a fragment I freely gave away, under the guise of mature duty and fiscal responsibility.

I became ill, wasted away, lost interest in life, lost the will to go on. The doctors called it Epstein Barr. Most people call it Yuppie flu. I call it denying my soul.

David encouraged me to follow my bliss. He helped me retrieve the lost pieces of me, helped me become more whole.

And then he died. The doctors called it cardiac arrhythmia. Most people call it a heart attack. I call it heart-breaking.

Why did he die? Had he denied his soul its essential food under the guise of mature duty and fiscal responsibility?

He saved my life. How I wish I could have saved his life.

Aurora Winter

∂

And did you get what you wanted
from this life, even so?
I did.
And what did you want?
To call myself beloved,
to feel myself beloved on the earth.

RAYMOND CARVER

Struggling and Soaring with Angels

David Doodles

David always used to doodle. Such neat but artistic, squarish capital letters. The alphabet. Kind of like this: ABCDEF. Letters touching, overlapping. But usually not all in one row. More in a corner. And mazes, sort of. A maze of letters. I wish I had some of his doodles. Perhaps they would speak volumes.

&

Ask and it will be given to you,
knock and the door will be opened to you.

MATTHEW 7:7

Aurora Winter

Son's Anger

Yale awakes angry. Accusations fly, "Why didn't you put out my clothes? Why didn't you get me Crunchios?"

I haven't yet showered or had my coffee, and I am under attack. The day is off to a bad start.

"I don't want to take a bath! I don't want to wash my hair!" He throws a cup of water onto the floor.

I snap. He cries.

I gather him in my arms, heedless of getting wet. Then, I gather some calmness, wrap him in a towel, and think as I rock him.

Last night, he roughhoused for hours with his uncle. This morning, the house is quiet. It's just the two of us. Once again.

"Are you angry because Daddy's not here to play with you any more?"

Yale clings to me, tearful.

I tell him, "It's okay to be angry. Or sad. Or mad."

Validated, he melts in my arms.

"But," I tease, "you take your chances if you pick on me before I've had my morning coffee."

He grins, "Mommy loves coffee!"

"Yes, I do." I give him a noisy smooch on his shoulder. "But not as much as I love you."

The kiss must have dislodged the chip on his shoulder, because he was his adorable, loving self for the rest of the day.

Struggling and Soaring with Angels

&

We can do no great things—only small things with great love.

MOTHER TERESA

Aurora Winter

"Cozzels"

Cozzels: a coined word meaning, "to cozy up to you and snuggle." Usually a noun, as in, "give you cozzels"—but not always, as in, "I'll cozzel you up."

A silly, made-up word, its frequent usage reflecting the happy warmth of our love.

&

*For in the dew of little things
the heart finds its morning and is refreshed.*

KAHLIL GIBRAN

Struggling and Soaring with Angels

Mirage

I feel lost without David. I've always followed him. Uncertain, tentative, even reluctant and afraid, I followed him. I trusted him. His life, his choices, were gilded. I teased him, calling him, "Midas Touch."

But somewhere, his unfailing propensity to attract the right thing, to intuitively leap to the right decision with incomplete information, started to slip away.

The last year or year and a half was filled with unexpected grief from life. A business sold—then boomeranged back. A quick choice to cut corners and rent a hovel "for a few months" that stretched into a very, very long year without a home, a nest. So important to me, so important to my Cancerian soul-mate.

A dream house that wouldn't stay on budget, that seemed a tantalizing mirage. We were in the desert, parched for a home, a new life, a new start. The mirage beckoned, then receded, taunting, teasing.

To protect myself from further pain, I distanced myself from our dream. Created a part of me that was resigned to never reaching the mirage. I grieve that David saw my detachment, and was perhaps hurt by it. I still cleaved to our dream. I thought I would have that priceless moment of crossing the threshold with him, holding his hand as we moved into our new home—into our new life together.

Aurora Winter

☙

A fool is happy when his cravings are satisfied.
A warrior is happy without reason.
That's what makes happiness the ultimate discipline.

DAN MILLMAN

Struggling and Soaring with Angels

Paralysis

Tasks which once had been easy now seem impossible. I can't seem to comprehend how to do the taxes (this from a woman who designed a tax shelter). Paying bills seems an impossible challenge.

Today, Bryce and I go shopping. We look at faucets and sinks and toilets and finishing touches for the house. Once, this task would have been a pleasure. Now, it's an onerous chore. My mind shies away from making the simplest choice. We shop all day and buy nothing, decide nothing. My brother is very patient with me, but I'm losing patience with myself.

I force myself to make a decision and choose a black tub and black sink for the master bedroom. I phone in the order, then instantly regret the decision. But what color other than black belongs in that bedroom?

&

Life is difficult.
This is a great truth, one of the greatest truths.
It is a great truth because once we truly see
this truth, we transcend it.
Once we truly know that life is difficult
—once we truly understand and accept it
—then life is no longer difficult.

M. SCOTT PECK

Aurora Winter

Car Accident

I can't find my keys. I search for fifteen minutes, looking high and low, frustrated to the point of tears. Finally I find them more or less where I always keep them.

Just as the sun is setting, I pull out to turn left across Lonsdale, a very steep street. Hidden by the hill and the glare is an oncoming car. It strikes us on the driver's side.

My Toyota Forerunner lurches, hit from below, and the wheels on the driver's side lift completely off the ground. I wait, more curious than afraid, to see if the car's momentum would roll us upside-down.

But the Forerunner is heavy, and the car that hit us is not. Gravity wins, and we drop back down onto all four wheels. I pull to the side of the road.

A policeman gives me a ticket. Firemen give Yale a stuffed Dalmatian. God gives me a reminder of my most precious cargo—my son.

I don't think it was coincidence that the car struck out at me. I don't care, don't feel worth saving. But whatever hits me, hits Yale. I have to be more careful. For his sake, I have to care.

&

Just to be is a blessing. Just to live is holy.

RABBI ABRAHAM HESCHEL

Struggling and Soaring with Angels

Dorothy: a Gift from God

After the car accident, I realize I need help. I already talk to my mother every day, and she has been endlessly patient and supportive. She visits frequently, and makes wonderful, wholesome meals.

She's going through a hard time herself right now. She feels thrown away by my father. They're in the midst of a bitter divorce. Before David died, I had championed my mother's case to my father. Now, I leave that to my two brothers. I try to listen patiently and lovingly to her heartaches, but I'm running on empty. I don't have much to give right now. We're both like birds with broken wings, and sometimes it's just too much brokenness. Even so, I crave her wisdom and her unconditional love.

She's living alone in a rented apartment, devastated by the death of her marriage. Yale and I are living in this roomy townhouse, traumatized by David's death.

Hungry for the stability and nurturing she brings, I ask her if she would consider moving in with us.

She agrees. Thank God.

&

Things don't fall apart. Things hold.
Lines connect in thin ways that last and last, and lives
become generations made out of pictures and words just kept.

LUCILLE CLIFTON

Aurora Winter

Liberty

I paid bills today! I never thought I'd be filled with such a sense of joy, of freedom, of triumph at paying bills! Less than a dozen paid—but sweet liberty!

&

If you can't do great things,
do small things in a great way.
Don't wait for great opportunities.
Seize common, everyday ones and make them great.

NAPOLEON HILL

Struggling and Soaring with Angels

Fastrack

Today, my reluctant teammate and I tidy the house. Yale disappears, and I find him in the living room, staring at Daddy's picture, his face wet with silent tears.

I wrap him in my arms, and we both look at the picture: Mommy and daddy on a sailboat. His father's face is freckled and ruddy from the sun: he's grinning broadly and pouring champagne. We've just launched our new boat—*Fastrack*. We admire his "handsome daddy," and I tell him about that day, tell him about his father winning Whidby Island Race Week, tell him about times we three sailed together on that boat.

Finally, Yale notices that the champagne isn't going into the glass I hold. Daddy missed. We share a laugh. (Jeff, a good friend with a sense of humor chose that photo to frame.)

It's time to get back to work. With a note of urgent desperation, Yale asks if he could please play Nintendo. I agree, and he's incredibly relieved. He wishes that Daddy was still alive to play 'Mario' with him.

Yale escapes to another reality, and so do I. I straighten the photo, flooded with happy memories. I remember the day David asked my permission to buy that boat. I remember saying that boats were a big hole in the water to pour money into, especially race boats, and that we didn't need to own another boat—we had plenty in inventory— we owned a yacht sales company.

My husband pulled me onto his lap, and agreed with my logic. But he wanted that C&C 37R, nonetheless.

Aurora Winter

I melted. "If you really, *really* want it, you can have it."

His face lit up with a delighted smile. I'm so glad that we bought that boat.

&

*Live so that you don't look back and
regret that you've wasted your life....
Life honestly and fully. Live.*

ELIZABETH KUBLER-ROSS

Struggling and Soaring with Angels

Just Checking

Nausea. Queasiness. A bloated feeling. 132 pounds—I haven't weighed this much since I was pregnant. Stabbing backache. Hope. Fast hummingbird wings of fear. A clinging to meaning, some sort of meaning. A rash wish to hold on. Undaunted by three miserly periods, I buy a pregnancy test kit.

My heart flutters. Hope mingles with fear. It could be a David-son or a David-daughter. But who would walk the infant up and down, up and down with endless patience like David did? Who would change the first diaper like David did? Who would stand by me, help me through labor, like David did?

But the test result is negative. I don't know how to feel. Another crushing letting go. Another challenge, another blessing spared.

&

I'm an old man who has known a great many problems,
most of which never happened.

MARK TWAIN

Aurora Winter

Poisonous Questions

Demons rise up from my depths and fire poisonous questions at me. Lethal questions.

Why didn't I get a mover? Why didn't I help him more? Why did I pressure him about money? Why was I so obsessed with my career?

Why, why, why? Why did you slip away in the middle of the night? My darling, I ache for you.

&

Be patient toward all that is unsolved in your heart,
and learn to love the questions themselves, like locked rooms
and like books that are written in a very foreign tongue.
Do not seek the answers, which cannot be given you
because you would not be able to live them.

RAINER MARIA RILKE

Struggling and Soaring with Angels

The Argument

How could I have let this happen? How can he be dead? How can he leave me with all these alligators churning, twisting and turning in a bitter, curdled fluid in the pit of my stomach? A roiling knot of guilt.

I'm so angry. Angry at him for abandoning me. But mostly infuriated with myself. I'm the one who should be dead, not him. Why didn't he stick around? Why did he leave me? Is it my fault? No, no, no, that's unthinkable. That's intolerable.

Alligators, yes; sins, yes; sorrows, yes. I freely admit I'm not perfect. But I did *not* kill him.

I'm so furious with myself, I want to choke the life out of me, see my eyes bulge with pain and suffocation.

Yet I want to forgive myself for letting him be in a place where he decided, *I'm outta here.* Forgive myself for letting him die.

I should have seen this coming. I ought to have averted this disaster. I should have saved him. But did I? No.

I thirst for revenge. I want to shriek and scream and lunge at my husband's murderer, pummel myself into the ground and wrestle my own head into the mud, scrape it along the gravel until it bleeds.

I did not kill him. I did *not!*

Aurora Winter

136

&

If you feel guilty,
you will insist on being punished in some way;
it feels good temporarily to relieve the guilt.
Mistakes call only for correction,
never punishment.

CHUCK SPEZZANO

Struggling and Soaring with Angels

More Guilt

I grapple with this rough-skinned monster. Pit its muscles and sinew against mine. Claws rake my soul. Its head thrashes, teeth slash me.

If I could just get a proper grip on it, if I could just stare straight into its cruel reptile eyes, perhaps I could defeat it. Perhaps. But it's powerful, vicious, relentless. It's a fight to the death. Or life.

&

Guilt is the great flypaper of Life.
We use it to hold ourselves back.
Guilt is...the excuse not to live fully
for fear of making another mistake.

CHUCK SPEZZANO

Aurora Winter

Nausea

Choking nausea. I am not comfortable within myself.

&

Be humble, for you are made of earth.
Be noble, for you are made of stars.

PROVERB

Struggling and Soaring with Angels

Courage

Courage, brave heart. Courage.
You are more than the love you shared.
You are more than your reflection in his admiring eyes.
Courage.

&

*With courage you will dare to take risks,
have the strength to be compassionate
and the wisdom to be humble.*

KESHAVAN NAIR

Aurora Winter

Hope

Hope springs up, spreading like leaping flames.

It seems to come from nowhere, from the smallest, most insignificant spark. Yet it catches hold and spreads like a summer forest fire, fanned by warm winds.

I've had blissful intimacy. Now is the time for personal growth, creation, discovery, rebirth.

&

I like living.
I have sometimes been wildly,
despairingly, acutely miserable,
racked with sorrow,
but through it all I still know
quite certainly that just to be alive
is a grand thing.

AGATHA CHRISTIE

Struggling and Soaring with Angels

His Birthday

That was a complete disaster. I had been looking forward to honoring David on his birthday. I had visions of spending a cozy time with his family and mine, nestled in the house that he built. Celebrating David's life. Ha!

For one thing, the house is far from finished. It's uninhabitable. But that defeat was partly offset by the kindness of my Whistler neighbor, Maureen, who said we were welcome to use her cabin.

I tried to slip next door with Yale to have a small ceremony honoring David on his birthday, but then everyone joined me, and it turned into a "command performance." We stood or sat on the cold plywood floor in the living room of the house that David built. I suggested, like Native Indians passing the peace pipe, that we each take a turn to speak some words in tribute to David.

It started off okay, then went horribly wrong. It ended with tears, slamming doors and David's father and brothers storming off, outraged.

My mother and one sister-in-law rallied to my support, while another sister-in-law played mediator.

I still don't know exactly what I did that was so deeply offensive. But I do know I would have been permanently shunned from my husband's family from this day forward, had it not been for Yale. Their love for Yale and fear of losing him kept tongues—if not tempers—somewhat in check. I don't think I did anything so unforgivable—except that their son is dead—and I'm not.

Aurora Winter

142

ॐ

Risk! Risk anything!
Care no more for the opinions of others,
for those voices.
Do the hardest thing on earth for you.
Act for yourself. Face the truth.

KATHERINE MANSFIELD

Struggling and Soaring with Angels

Berenstain Bears Interrupted

I tuck Yale into bed, and read his favorite Berenstain Bears books to him.

The phone rings, and it's long distance from a dear friend, so I take it. Maura was flying into Rome on David's birthday and saw someone who resembled David so much that she almost threw up. She stared at him, even followed him through customs to see his passport and make absolutely certain it wasn't David.

In his bedroom, Yale is crying. I hang up quickly.

"My Dad," Yale sobs.

I comfort him, "It's okay, honey. Mommy's here."

"There are some good things about Dad being dead, and there are some bad things. The good thing is we can stay up late and do things Dad doesn't like us to do. The bad thing is—it's not much fun without Dad."

So true. I encourage Yale to talk and cry. I tell him there are good things and bad things about most things.

&

Listening is a form of accepting.

STELLA MANN

Aurora Winter

This Widow Business
Is Getting Boring

This widow business is getting boring. There's no
longer the life-threatening, overwhelming surge of
dramatic emotions. I miss David, and I'm a bit annoyed
with him, I'll admit, but I'm not so furious anymore.

I feel sort of dead, though. Am I burying something,
which is deadening me...or am I always going to feel like
this without love?

&

The agonies, the mad midnight moments,
must, in the course of nature, die away.
But what will follow?
Just this apathy, this dead flatness? ...
Does grief finally subside
into boredom tinged by faint nausea?

C. S. LEWIS

Struggling and Soaring with Angels

Accused

I stand accused. I am plaintiff, defendant, judge, and jury. But mostly, I am the blood-thirsty mob, shouting accusations. Each accusation drives like a nail through my flesh. Each thought stings like a whip and draws blood.

The judge finds no grounds for execution and offers instead a known murderer. But the mob refuses reason. Demanding the real criminal be pardoned, the irate mob turns on me, chanting, "Crucify her! Crucify her!" Their shouts are deafening. They refuse to be placated.

The meek defendant enters a guilty plea. Like Pontius Pilot, the judge has little choice. Releasing the real murderer, the judge declares me guilty.

I can't bear the crushing weight of this cross. Pouring vinegar into my wounds, shouting taunts, merciless, I crucify myself.

&

Father, forgive them,
for they do not know what they are doing.

JESUS, QUOTED IN LUKE 23:34

Aurora Winter

IV. Temptations

Armed with experience with stormy weather,
I stride purposefully out into the day.
Mixed sun and rain is forecast,
and I know I can handle it, come what may,
I've purchased an umbrella!
Sometimes, I step into a puddle
which turns out to be a surprisingly deep pothole,
and I stumble and get wet and muddy.
Oh, well. I guess I need boots.

Struggling and Soaring with Angels

The Psychic

Guilt turns and turns within me, like some green crocodile roiling inside me. Nastier than bile, gnawing on me from the inside.

I killed my husband. I knew I did! If only I'd been a better wife. If only I'd realized the stress he'd been under. If only we'd hired a mover. If only I'd known better CPR. If only the phone had been connected. If only I hadn't abandoned him to follow my dream of being a writer. If only I'd immediately spurned the flattering attentions of my mentor.

My mind seizes upon this last. That must have been the final blow. How could I accept all these well-meaning condolences when I knew I'd killed him?

An irregular heartbeat? That's no reason to die. This must be my fault.

I want to die. But that option is out. I'm not going to leave our son an orphan. But this guilt is unbearable. I need some relief. In desperation, I consult a psychic.

She tells me I'm going to meet three men.

I brush that aside—I don't care about men. I share my anguish. Did I somehow cause David's death?

"You're not God. His death isn't about you, it's about him. He had his own destiny, his own life—his own death," the psychic says.

With trepidation, I blurt out my infidelity.

She laughs at the absurdity. "A stolen kiss, a moment's confusion— that's not infidelity." She dismisses my earnest self-accusation and chides me to get a proper sense of

Aurora Winter

perspective. "What protégé wouldn't be confused when her Mentor tells her he loves her? It happens on movie sets so frequently, it's cliché. The thrill of creating something together is mistaken for something else, when all it is about is the joy of creation and the sweet taste of success. You didn't have sex. It didn't go anywhere. You told him you loved your husband and your son and would never leave them. Let it go."

But my heart's crushing burden is not so easily dislodged. "How do I know David didn't leave this planet because he felt me leaving him?"

The psychic smiles sagely. She challenges my perceptions. "How do you know you didn't feel attracted to your Mentor because you felt your husband leaving you?"

Paradigm shift.

&

There is something distinguished about even his failures;
they sink not trivially, but with a certain air of majesty,
like a great ship, its flags flying, full of holes.

GEORGE JEAN NATHAN

The Miracle of Friendship

It's my birthday, and I feel blessed by so many friends and family members. David's death was like an earthquake, and the ground shook and cracked open under my feet. By all rights, I should have fallen into the crevice and perished.

The love of my family and friends has been like a spider web—almost invisible, yet incredibly strong. It is this web of love that caught me and kept me from falling. So I remain upright and standing, no ground under my feet, yet securely held in place by many strands of love.

&

*There is nothing on this earth
more to be prized than true friendship.*

SAINT THOMAS AQUINAS

Aurora Winter

Mocking Death

I meet a man on a plane, "Randy," a machinist who writes poetry. He kisses me when I'm half asleep. Before my mind wakes up enough to say no, my body says yes.

Leaving the plane, the elevator ride turns breathless, steamy. He unabashedly suggests we get a hotel room. I'm shocked by his audacity.

We walk in the gray rain. Chilly gusts of wind curl around us, but I'm warm.

I want to know if he'll turn psycho when the door is shut and tightly locked like my heart. Warn him not to fall in love with me.

I want to know how he feels about safe sex. But my hands are all over him. He feels great to me.

I want to know if he'll respect a no, but my body trembles with yes.

Questions pose themselves in my head, but my brain is disconnected from my tongue.

He gets annoyed at me for making him do all the talking.

Underneath the railway bridge, he passionately embraces me. My knees nearly buckle, fireworks explode.

He looks at me in astonishment.

Like a colt, I shake my mane. Energy flies.

Struggling and Soaring with Angels

&

You will do foolish things,
but do them with enthusiasm.

COLETTE

Aurora Winter

Out of Body Experience

The doors burst open
and the hurricane enters
with him.

My mind is blown back
so far it doesn't even
observe
as my body trembles
in ecstasy.

The storm rages inside me,
dark and wet.
Thunder, lightening, tornadoes.
I can't contain it.

So I become the storm.
Insatiable, yet
satisfied already.

&

Don't sigh, don't yawn, seek passion, passion, passion.

RUMI

Struggling and Soaring with Angels

Emotional Cripple

I'm a tangled tumble of emotions. I worked out three times today to try to work through this. Lesson: you can't get near another human being without the risk of hurt feelings, no matter what is said beforehand.

I didn't want to give anyone the power to hurt me again. I want to be defiant, alone, proud, needing nothing, needing no one.

But my feelings will be hurt if Randy doesn't call me. And if he doesn't, it's because I hurt his feelings (without meaning to).

Two hypersensitive people pretending to be cool in our aloneness. Something else in common.

How can I have so much in common with someone who is nothing like my soul mate? I hate this. I'm enraged at David for dying. I want to sell everything, run away, shuck all my responsibilities. I want to shirk my body, rise up, be freed. My life is a meaningless burden of responsibilities.

&

*You may have a fresh start any moment you choose,
for this thing we call "failure"
is not the falling down, but the staying down.*

MARY PICKFORD

Aurora Winter

Sleepover

Randy called. We get together, and he complains about having to drag everything out of me. How's that for a sexual stereotype role reversal?

When we have sex, it's as though the forces of Life and Death battle, and the battlefield is my body. Foaming with sweat and blood, warhorses scream as they lash out with their teeth and hooves. Hooves clatter, swords clang, armor is pierced. Death's black horse and rider are forced to retreat by this ferocious, intense onslaught of undiluted Life.

Afterwards, he tells me he's going to have sex only with me. I react defensively. Instead of agreeing, I turn into a porcupine and tell him he can do whatever he wants. I'm going to do whatever I want.

He seems hurt by my retort. He lets his commitment stand, in spite of my lack of reciprocation. I'm not planning on having sex with anyone else, but I can't bring myself to spit out those words. That feels like commitment, feels like danger, feels like a trap.

I sleep over at his house for the first time. Every time he breathes deeply, I wake up, heart racing, panicked that he's dying.

The last time I slept with a man, he didn't wake up.

Struggling and Soaring with Angels

&

The best way out is always through.

ROBERT FROST

Aurora Winter

Mirror, Mirror

We have nothing in common.
We don't travel in the same circles.
We don't have the same background.

And yet—he's my mirror.
He wants everything/wants nothing
is defiantly self-sufficient/lonely
is terrified of intimacy/craves intimacy—
just like me.

Extremes.
There's a rawness to him.
He's not like anyone
I've ever had in my life, before.
He's not like anyone
I would have chosen in my life, before.

And neither am I.

&

The garden of the world has no limits except in your mind.
Its presence is more beautiful than the stars,
With more clarity than the polished mirror of your heart.

RUMI

Struggling and Soaring with Angels

Magnet

The part of my mind that observes everything and takes notes is intrigued. After lying dormant for months, my answering machine is now constantly winking. Suddenly, I'm a man-magnet. It's the siren call of a female in heat.

Feeling like a woman scorned, I mutiny. I feel compelled to prove I'm desirable. Prove I'm alive. Prove that David made a mistake.

&

It is better to be looked over than overlooked.

MAE WEST

Aurora Winter

Returning to the Hospital

I'm out with a girlfriend, and I feel uneasy. *Is Yale okay?* I call the babysitter, and am assured, "He's fine. Everything's fine."

I return to my girlfriend, but I can't shake this uneasy feeling. Apologizing, I cancel the evening so I can return to my son.

Minutes later, I pull into the driveway just as the babysitter is rushing my son out the door. "He can't breathe!"

Oh my God! I grab my son, and we race toward Lions Gate Hospital. Waves of memory assault me as I drive my slowly suffocating son to the hospital. He gasps for air...but I cannot find the way. It is blocked by the last time I took this journey.

My husband in the back of the ambulance, me in front. "Hold on, David! Hold on!" my desperate plea fades to a mere murmur. On some level, I know.

My friend tells me where to turn. She parks my Forerunner. Alone, I carry my only son through the fateful doors marked: Emergency.

Yale chokes on air. I am deathly calm.

The nurse hustles us in, "Is his father coming?"

"His father is dead." I do not add that he was pronounced dead mere feet from where I stand.

Yale hacks, breaking dozens of blood vessels in his face. He throws up all over me. I don't care.

An oxygen mask is clamped on; he's rushed to x-ray. Is something blocking his airways? Nothing physical, I know.

Struggling and Soaring with Angels

I don't leave his side. Shielded by lead, I hold his hand, hold his trust.

He lies still for the x-ray. Then he writhes in panic and fights to remove the mask of life. I pick up my five-year-old like a baby. A rocking chair appears. I rock him, swaddling him in my cocoon of safety.

He relaxes.

I answer questions like a computer. Learning that Yale and I just have each other, the doctor softens.

I stay in my frozen fortress. This terror feels too familiar. I'm not comforted by the medical bustle around us, but rather by the icy thought that if Yale dies, I can blow my head off.

The epinephrine takes hold, and Yale falls asleep against my breast. His chest rises and falls in a sweet, gentle rhythm.

He's assigned a bed in pediatrics. I'm prepared to fight to stay by his side, but no one challenges me.

A lioness, I lie beside him, guarding his every breath. All night long.

&

I'll never let you go, Mommy.
And you never let me go, either.
We'll hold on to each other, forever.

MATTIE J. T. STEPANEK

Aurora Winter

The Croup

What caused the croup? Was it my hectic schedule, out almost every night? Was it my yearning to be free, my plans to escape to Thailand for a month without my son?

Was it my sense of being suffocated by the constant demands of being a single mom?

Was this a call, an urgent reminder, that he needs me? That he can't breathe without me?

I cancel my plans to go away for the weekend. I cancel my plans to go to Thailand. I cancel my sense of feeling suffocated.

I won't leave my son's side. He's my most precious burden. The doctors are amazed by how quickly he recovers.

I am not.

&

Love is the heartbeat of all of life.

PARAMAHANSA YOGANANDA

Struggling and Soaring with Angels

Rush

It wasn't just about the rush of
mainlining ecstasy,
though it started out that way
...or did it?

I felt I recognized your bright eyes
from another time and place.

You released the storm within me
into passion, not bitterness.
You opened a locked door
...and I walked through.

It was a true gift
and more than enough.

But...your light burns so brightly,
you chase your dreams with such passion
(and you feel so good, smell so good)
that I wanted more.

A piece of your heart
(just a small piece).

Aurora Winter

For me, love equaled pain,
I wanted no part of that game.
But I craved your affection
...not getting love was also pain.
Ahh...bitter double bind.

Then, perhaps, I was cruel.
Your body is so hot,
but your heart seems so cool.
Starving for some simple affection,
I dated other guys, told you everything.

You pretended not to care.
I pretended I might sleep with them.

Then, you seemed to soften,
seemed truly happy to see me,
and I relaxed,
prepared to be content.

And then you stood me up.
Didn't phone...weren't at home.
I passed through anger...to anguished fear.
I called the hospitals...I tortured myself.
But you were with her.

I was shattered.
I named you Coward.

Struggling and Soaring with Angels

The missing puzzle piece slapped in my face,
but now I understand us both.
It's cowardice that makes us seek
self-defeating relationships.

So we can pretend we don't care.
But it hurts, it hurts anyway.

You accuse me of wanting to change you,
and I confess you're right.
I want to heal you,
just as I let you heal me.

Don't endlessly repeat the same lesson.
It's not your woman you starve
for love, but your Self.

Choose whom to love wisely,
then brave heart, throw caution to the wind.
As you love her, and she loves you, and
fueled by love, each will love the other more intensely,
forming an infinite loop of love,
a beaming, healing perpetual motion love machine.

&

*Fortunately analysis is not the only way to resolve inner conflicts.
Life itself still remains a very effective therapist.*

KAREN HORNEY

Aurora Winter

My Guides

The psychic teaches me how to meditate and about guides, guardian angels I can call upon when I'm meditating. My female guide isn't quite human. She's rippling with muscles ...and she has a tail. My male guide, Aaron, smolders with beauty. Dark curls frame his boyish face.

I ask them what I need to know, and they say, "Love thyself." Talking to them seems a harmless way of connecting with fragments of myself. Soon, I know them intimately, which is not surprising, as they're just parts of me. Or are they?

I attend a conference at a film festival and am floored when I actually *meet* "Aaron." When we shake hands, a spark of electricity passes between us. "Aaron" is a brilliant screenwriter. I admire his work—in fact, I had previously decided to emulate the flawless structure of one of his feature films. He invites me to the screening of his new film and tries to pass tickets to me for the party afterwards, but his attempt is thwarted by the throng. In a grand gesture, he invites the entire theatre to the wrap party—just so I can attend.

Later, he invites me to his hotel room. We have grapes and champagne, kiss, and talk about philosophy and death. Roles are oddly reversed, as I seem to be the sage, while he seems to be the fumbling adolescent.

I don't understand. How can someone who exists only in my mind turn out to be a real person?

Struggling and Soaring with Angels

இ

*I want to know God's thoughts
...the rest are details.*

ALBERT EINSTEIN

Aurora Winter

The Third Man

I meet the third man the Psychic predicted. He's gentle, non-judgmental, playful, and healing. Jacques is the host of a TV show, an actor, writer, and masseuse. He massages my hand, and it turns into butter. I didn't realize how much tension I've been holding in my body.

Jacques can make up rhyming, silly songs on the spot, so of course Yale is enchanted.

&

Avoiding danger is no safer
in the long run than outright exposure.
The fearful are caught as often as the bold.

HELEN KELLER

Struggling and Soaring with Angels

Chez Toi

Your hands knead me
gently, then painfully deep.
Your voice paints pictures—
sparkling green water caresses.
I relax, yet sparks tingle.
Knowing I'm not supposed to,
I open my eyes.

Shrouded in black tresses,
dragon eyes burn into mine.
I am enthralled.
Wanting to captive you,
I gallop with unbridled abandon
on the borders of intimacy.

Then, I feel so vulnerable.
As though I'd laid
my soul
bare for you to see.
I stand trembling in a gale
...ready to bolt.

We can only learn to love by loving.

IRIS MURDOCH

Aurora Winter

The Urn

The urn stayed at the funeral home for a long time. Finally, David's brother picked it up. Months later, I asked for it and took it home.

Once I got over an initial awkwardness, I had many pleasant chats with my husband. I found the cold, smooth, golden surface of the urn comforting. I liked the substantial weight of it.

Today, I decided to share the urn with my son. I tell Yale that after Daddy was cremated, they put what was left of his body into this urn.

"What's cremated?" Yale asks.

I couldn't bring myself to say that his body was burned, I didn't want my son to have fiery nightmares. So I explain, "Cremation is the process which took all the water out of Daddy's body, leaving just the dust behind."

"Is Daddy in there?" he asks.

"No, Daddy's soul is with us always, watching over us, floating free in the air. But what is left of Daddy's body is in here."

With the innocence of a five-year-old, Yale asks, "Can I see inside?"

I'd never actually opened the urn, and my stomach flops at the suggestion, but I agree and unscrew the lid. Inside the beautiful golden urn is a plastic bag containing his father's ashes. "See—Daddy's ashes."

"Can I feel them?"

My stomach knots, but I think, it's his father, it's his process. Who am I to question the wisdom of a child?

Struggling and Soaring with Angels

Didn't Jesus say to be as little children? So I say, "Okay," and open the plastic bag.

Yale dips his fingers into the soft, fine ashes and seems satisfied. I close the bag, close the urn.

His questions and his curiosity satisfied, he slides off my lap, content, and goes to play.

And I marvel at my little teacher.

&

I tell you the truth, unless you change
and become like little children,
you will never enter the kingdom of heaven.

JESUS, QUOTED IN MATTHEW 18:3

Aurora Winter

The First Christmas without Him

"What do you want for Christmas?" I ask Yale.

"A baby brother," he replies, without skipping a beat.

"What—not a sister?" I say, stalling for time.

"No. I want a baby brother."

"For one thing, honey, you can't choose whether it's a baby brother or a baby sister. And for another thing, a baby needs a daddy, and you can't have a baby brother (or even a baby sister) without a daddy. So I'm sorry, you can't have a baby brother for Christmas."

My five-year-old is disappointed. "I want a baby brother to play with."

"Babies aren't that much fun to play with, anyway. Not at first. What else would you like for Christmas?"

That's a question that gets a five-year-old's full attention. Yale excitedly gives me a long wish list.

Later, I have a lot of fun shopping and buy every single thing on his wish list (except the baby brother). I label his presents "from Santa," "from Mom," and even "from Dad." I probably shouldn't have put gifts "from Dad." But I can't face a Christmas tree with no presents for my son from his father.

Martha Stewart would be proud. The Christmas tree is beautiful...and at its feet is a cornucopia of abundance. But even so, I'm afraid that it won't be enough. How could it ever be enough?

Struggling and Soaring with Angels

171

But on Christmas morning, my five-year-old is all smiles, giggles and excited shrieks of delight. After opening his main gift, he literally bowls me over with his gratitude and enthusiasm. It is enough.

It is more than enough.

&

I have enough for this life.
If there is no other life,
then this one has been enough
to make it worth being born.

PEARL S. BUCK

Aurora Winter

Cellular Scream

Three-hundred-and-sixty-four days have gone by. The hours tick by. At four a.m. tomorrow morning, it will be exactly one year since David died.

One whole year. It feels like five. When he died, I naively thought I'd be okay in a year. I'd have "gotten over it."

This is not the kind of thing you get over. Not ever. But I thought at least I'd feel healed, a bit more healed. A year is an awfully long time. Yet it's not.

I don't feel healed. I feel raw and vulnerable. I sit by the fire, shivering, though it's not cold. A blanket is offered, and I snuggle in it for warmth, but this is the kind of chill that neither a fire, nor a blanket, nor hot chocolate can dispel.

As the evening progresses, I'm overcome by a powerful sense of dread. It doesn't matter that I'm not alone. It doesn't matter that I tell myself, *There's nothing to be afraid of.*

My cells tremble with dread. They seem to be trying to scream. The trauma of my husband dying beside me has been engraved upon my very cells.

A stupor overcomes me. I cannot even make it up the stairs unaided.

Struggling and Soaring with Angels

&

Do not be desirous of having things done quickly.
Do not look at small advantages.
Desire to have things done quickly
prevents their being done thoroughly.
Looking at small advantages prevents
great affairs from being accomplished.

CONFUCIUS

Aurora Winter

V. TRIUMPH

The weather is predominantly fair.
A spring in my step, I venture boldly outside
and delight in the sunshine. Sometimes,
Mother Nature sends a rogue storm my way,
and I get caught outside with neither umbrella nor boots.
Oh, well, no big deal. I've been soaked and muddy before,
and I survived. More than survived—I thrived.
Now, I know the sun will rise again tomorrow,
and the forecast, just as in Southern California,
will most likely be sunny and fair.

Struggling and Soaring with Angels

My Lesson

Eli's Lesson is being produced. I'm a not a "wannabe" writer any more—I'm a produced screenwriter. The script I researched and co-wrote attracts an Oscar-winning star. Drawn to the heartwarming screenplay, Jack Palance says, "It's a beautiful story. It's a beautiful message. There's a line in it in which I say, 'to let your dreams die because others say it can't be done is a terrible thing.' It is a terrible thing, not just in the film, but anywhere."

I'm star-struck when Jack Palance brings me roses and buys me breakfast. I can hardly believe I'm having blueberry pancakes with a legend—a legend who stars in *my* movie. It seems surreal.

On set in Regina, I'm wide-eyed with wonder. It's three a.m. and bitterly cold. But nothing can take away the warm glow of satisfaction in my heart as I watch the director, cast, and crew shooting the film's climactic scene. No expense has been spared to create what I saw in my mind's eye.

In spite of incredible odds, Eli achieves his heart's desire. In a magical moment, he actually flies. He's ecstatic, emboldened, transformed. In a surprise twist, he finds a way to reconcile his seemingly-impossible dream of being a pilot with the demands of being a Hutterite. Eli returns home, delighted by the unexpected opportunity to become the first-ever Hutterite crop duster.

In spite of incredible odds, I achieve *my* heart's desire—I become a produced screenwriter. I'm ecstatic, emboldened,

Aurora Winter

transformed. In a surprise twist, writing *Eli's Lesson* catapults me from obscurity into the limelight. Several magazines and newspapers profile me. *Eli's Lesson* sweeps the globe and wins several awards.

Maybe God doesn't hate me after all. Maybe my dreams of writing aren't absurd. Maybe God has a plan for me and is leading me. Guided by this encouragement, I renew my commitment to my dreams.

The message in *Eli's Lesson* is that no dream is truly impossible, no matter what the odds, if it's burning deep within your soul. To let your dreams die because others say it can't be done *is* a terrible thing.

To let your dreams die because someone you love dies is to let your soul die and turn one tragedy into two. That was *my* lesson. I realize that the person who most needed the message of hope in *Eli's Lesson*—was me.

&

Hope is grief's best music.

ANONYMOUS

Struggling and Soaring with Angels

Foundation

I dream that I'm in a big, beautiful house overlooking the water. My father visits, and I'm delighted to give him the grand tour. We go from room to room, and he admires my home as I swell with pride.

Finally, we reach the basement. There's not much to see here, but, wanting to be thorough, I open the door and flip on the light. The unadorned light bulbs reveal a plain, dark basement crammed with cardboard boxes. I'm about to shut the door when I notice the basement floor is damp. *What? That's not right.*

As we investigate, the trickle becomes a foot of water, and the boxes start to float. With alarm, I realize that the house must be built on a dry creek bed. Well, it's not dry any more. Soon, a creek flows through my basement. It swells and cannot be contained. The force of the water breaks through the concrete foundation as easily as if it had been made of paper. The rivulet sweeps the cardboard boxes out to sea.

Fearful for our lives, my father and I abandon my house and scramble to higher ground. Looking back at the house from a safe distance, we see a raging river churning through the basement, eroding the foundation, stripping away everything in its path. My beautiful home, which had seemed so solid and had been such a source of pride and joy, now precariously straddles a gaping chasm.

I can't move the river; that much is clear. Must I abandon my home? How can I reinforce the foundation when my home is built on a creek bed, built on sand?

Aurora Winter

But wait. The river licks away the sand, revealing, in some places, bedrock. Is there enough bedrock to support the house—or will it be swept away like the grains of sand?

&

Dreams are like letters from God.
Isn't it time you answered your mail?

MARIE LOUIS VON FRANZ

Struggling and Soaring with Angels

Acceptance

I meet my dead husband at the airport. We sit across from each other, and I unleash my fury, *How could you die beside me? How could you rip my heart out? How could you abandon me?*

I pound my fist on the cold, hard, cheap table, heedless of the faceless passersby, all heading purposefully somewhere else. My fury spent, my voice quavers as I confront him with his ultimate betrayal, *How could you leave our son without his father?*

Silently, compassionately, my husband listens to the outpourings of my raging heart. He does not take the baited hook, nor does he reach out to comfort me with his warm, strong hands. He reaches out to me in the only way he can—in this dream.

If you had it to do all over again, would you still marry me?

I think for a moment, flooded with joyful memories. Love shared, boats sailed, dreams achieved—together. I'd take my time with him, though it be short. *Yes.*

If you had it to do all over again, would you still have our son?

This time the answer is quicker, surer. I wouldn't give up our son for the world! He is the light of my life, my joy, my blessing. *Yes!*

Given that, would you want to know that I would die young?

His question gives me pause. Would I choose to taint our joy with dread? I look into my heart, and after a long moment, see the answer. *No.*

Aurora Winter

180

A sense of peace soothes my rage and my sorrow. I did not choose my fate. And yet—I would.

&

I've dreamt in my life dreams
that have stayed with me ever after,
and changed my ideas;
they've gone through and through me,
like wine through water,
and altered the color of my mind.

EMILY BRONTE

Struggling and Soaring with Angels

Widows, Orphans and Angry Men

Class Valedictorian, Vice-President of the Students' Council, champion of the 100 meter dash, honors student, privileged child of an academic family, world-traveled, university–educated. All these things are true.

But my identity doesn't seem to fit any more. Just as my clothes don't feel right. Just as the reflection in the mirror doesn't look right.

In the past, I'd been accused of being arrogant, aloof, standoffish. That's probably true, and I apologize to all I slighted. Now, things are different. Like attracts like, and I draw to me all manner of wounded souls.

My collection of "widows and orphans," as my mother ruefully observes. My closest female friends are both widows; one was raped as a child.

And the "boys" I have dated since my husband died have been so wounded. One, whose father left when he was only two, was gentle and sweet and passive. Another's mother died in his arms when he was fourteen, then his father kicked him out of the house. He was wounded and angry and aggressive. But isn't anger just the other side of fear? And wasn't I still so angry and afraid?

I didn't know these facts when I was first drawn to these friends and lovers (or they were drawn to me). But my wounded soul felt a resonance with their woundedness, and we picked each other infallibly. Our brokenness became our bond.

Aurora Winter

182

But—it's the flaw that makes the star in a sapphire. It's the crack in the vase that lets the light in. It's the chink in our armor that lets the love in.

ॐ

Everyone, like true brothers and sisters,
is bonded by pain and exists solely
to endure hardship and grow.

ELIZABETH KUBLER-ROSS

Struggling and Soaring with Angels

Miraculous Coincidences

I really don't want to go to the party. I feel a cold coming on, and I'd rather curl up in bed with a good book. But Jacques cajoles me into accompanying him, and I reluctantly tag along. Sipping my soda, I strike up a conversation with the man sitting beside me. I have no idea who he is, but he's in the film business, like most of the people here. I tell him about the movie I'm currently writing, *Lost Rituals*, about absent fathers and lost sons.

I'm surprised when he reveals that he's the head of the BC Film Commission. He asks me to represent the province at the upcoming Banff Television Festival and to pitch my movie in front of 400 or so industry executives.

I think, *You've got to be kidding. If I blow it, I'll humiliate myself in front of the entire film and television community, and I'll never work again!* But then I think, *Why not? I'm barely working now—or rather, I'm working a lot, but barely being paid—what have I got to lose?*

My stomach knots in protest, but I decide to embrace the opportunity, and I agree.

A couple of days later, a woman calls and introduces herself as Joanne. She's a documentary filmmaker, and she'd like to follow me around the Banff Television Festival to make a half-hour documentary for the CBC, focusing on my pitch at the market simulation.

Oh great, I think, *not only can I humiliate myself once in front of 400 or so of the most powerful and influential people in my industry, but then, if anyone missed it, they can watch it on national television.*

Aurora Winter

I confess I've never been on camera, I've never pitched a movie script to more than four people, and the last time I was speaking to an audience, I was teaching an aerobics class at Gold's Gym. I can't promise it'll be good television.

Undeterred by my doubts, Joanne insists that she wants me.

My stomach seems to be having seizures. But I decide, *Why not?*

Later, at the Banff Television Festival, I quickly get used to having the documentary crew follow me around and sometimes forget that my every word is being recorded.

The closer it gets to the time to go onstage and do my pitch, the more the words get jumbled up in my head. I'd lived and breathed this script for months and have woven it into a beautiful tapestry. In my head (or on paper), I liked to play with the threads and can smoothly weave the intersecting threads of plot and subplot and character in different, pleasing patterns, never getting tangled. But now, it is as if some alley cat had snarled everything. Twigs and bits of string and possibly some dead thing seem all matted up in the tapestry of the story in my mind.

Pacing in my room, I rehearse various pitches, and they all sound lame, long-winded and dull. My neck goes into spasm in protest and panic. I have to see a masseuse. *Why did I agree to this? What on earth possessed me?*

The big moment arrives. The moderator and I sit bathed in light on the podium. The camera crews roll film. The audience is live. Live people who really matter.

And now, when it really counts, somehow, incredibly— miraculously—the words flow. I'm "on." I tell the story of *Lost Rituals*, of absent fathers and lost sons, and how boys can be raised by mothers, but need men to turn into men.

Struggling and Soaring with Angels

Without fathers to mentor them, these boys try to mentor each other, with tragic results. The audience hushes, hanging on my every word, caring about those boys— caring about me.

And when the lights come up, the story sparks a bidding war. *Playback* reported, "Winter's *Lost Rituals* pitch created an all-out bidding frenzy. The coming-of-age story caused Michael Spivak (Vice-President Production at Global Television) to 'want to go all the way' on the project and sparked Gary Randall (Spelling Television President) to bid US$40,000 for the second draft, as did Ferns (with 'Spelling's money'). Dromgoole joined in the fray to link with Global against Randall, Ferns and the CTV Television Network."

My agent is thrilled to be fielding offers on my behalf. The documentary filmmaker is elated—she said she couldn't have scripted a more dramatic finish. The head of the BC Film Commission congratulates me. He says he never doubted that I would make him look good.

I'm euphoric. In my wildest dreams, I never dreamt it would go so well.

I guess I'll have to start having bigger dreams.

Aurora Winter

&

Until one is committed, there is hesitancy,
the chance to draw back,   always ineffectiveness.
Concerning all acts of initiative,
there is one elementary truth,
the ignorance of which kills countless ideas
and splendid plans: the moment one definitely
commits oneself, then Providence moves too.

W. H. MURRAY

Struggling and Soaring with Angels

Father's Day

Father's Day.
The whole happy celebration,
the inescapable bombardment
of ads and images
could hardly be more cruelly crafted
to tear the scab off old wounds
and make us bleed.

&

We shall draw from the heart of suffering itself
the means of inspiration and survival.

SIR WINSTON CHURCHILL

Aurora Winter

Moving to Whistler

I feel restless and decide to move from Vancouver to Whistler. It feels important to make the house that David built our home. It feels like time to cut the umbilical cord and stop living with my mother.

My vision of how wonderful our life will be in Whistler is in sharp contrast to the reality. Yale doesn't like skiing. Friends and family visit rarely. I feel isolated.

The house itself annoys me. Every time I turn around, I'm confronted by something else that wasn't finished or that doesn't work. When people visit, I feel ashamed of the painted concrete floor and the light fixtures that are bare bulbs. I feel compelled to apologize for the house's incompleteness and glaring imperfections.

&

*Restlessness is discontent,
and discontent is the first necessity of progress.*

THOMAS EDISON

Struggling and Soaring with Angels

More Miracles

The Canadian Film Center in Toronto accepts my application to take the producers' workshop. I hesitate to leave my son for four weeks, but Bonnie assures me that she'll take good care of him. I can't afford to stay in a hotel for that length of time, so I call one of the few people I know in Toronto, Victor. He's the reporter who profiled me in Maclean's magazine as one of "100 Canadians to Watch." Victor says that my timing is fortuitous. His cousin is going to be away on vacation when I'm in Toronto—I can stay in her lovely apartment. Fantastic.

In Toronto, I miss my son, but try to absorb everything I can about writing and producing film and television. A number of speakers address our group, including Seaton, the President of Canada's largest television production company, Atlantis.

At coffee break, heart racing, I stalk Seaton surreptitiously, then pounce at an opportune moment. We chat for a few moments, and I say I would like the opportunity to pitch my movie projects to him. I ask for a meeting. And then let the silence hang in the air. As the seconds tick by, I hear David's coaching, *The salesperson's most powerful tool is silence.*

And—Seaton invites me to breakfast. Wow.

At breakfast the following day, I'm so nervous that I can't shut up. I prattle on about my life, the yacht sales business, real estate—everything but pitching my two scripts. As the waiter clears the breakfast plates, I take a deep breath. I can't put this off any longer. I take the

Aurora Winter

plunge and pitch one script. After the pitch, there's silence for a moment. Finally, I can't bear it any longer, and I ask him if he would like to hear the pitch for my other movie. He says, no, not now.

Oh. What a disappointment. And then, miracle of miracles, he says something completely unexpected—he offers me a full-time job as his head of development.

Oh, my God! This is the most incredible opportunity, and a far better gift than having one of my movie scripts optioned.

Seaton wants to know if I'm interested. *Am I interested?* In spite of all the training David gave me in the art of salesmanship, it's all I can do not to blurt out that I'd work for free for the experience. With as much calm coolness as I can muster (which I'm sure isn't much as I'm completely transparent), I tell him, yes, I'm interested.

He excuses himself, he has to run, but tells me to make an appointment with his secretary, and we'll discuss the details of the job offer.

I'm so excited that I don't know what to do with myself. So I do what any woman would do under similar circumstances—I shop. I splurge and buy my very first Armani suit so I'll look like a television executive.

On my way to the follow-up meeting with Seaton, I can hear David's voice coaching me. *Ask open-ended questions. Probe. Always close for the next step. It's okay to say that you'll think about it.* I come up with a figure in my head. If he says less than that figure, I'll have to ask for more. I can't move 3,000 miles for less.

At the meeting, Seaton describes the job, and it sounds fantastic. I can't imagine a more wonderful boss. He has so much soul and is so creative. Finally, stomach clenched, I

Struggling and Soaring with Angels

casually ask what sort of salary figure he has in mind. Silence hangs in the air. David cautions me, *Don't say anything, don't say anything, don't say anything.*

And Seaton fills the silence with an answer. Oh. My. God. The salary is double what I expected. I tell Seaton I have to sleep on it and that I'll get back to him.

That night, I call my dad and ask his advice. Should I take the job? I'd have to move 3,000 miles, uproot Yale, I don't have a support network of friends and family in Toronto.

He says I've been offered a starting salary of more money than he earned with a Ph.D. as Chairman of the Department of Agricultural Economics at UBC. It's a great company, it's exactly what I want to do, I'll learn and meet a lot of people. Should I take the job? What's there to think about?

So I accept. I'm blessed with a prestigious job working for an incredibly creative, supportive boss. I cannot conceive of a faster, more exciting or more lucrative way to learn about all aspects of film and television, from the initial pitch through script development, casting, financing, production, marketing and international distribution. I'm given the gift of being able to support my little family of two—and reach for my dreams, too.

*It is impossible
on reasonable grounds
to disbelieve miracles.*

BLAISE PASCAL

Aurora Winter

THREE YEARS
THIRD ANNIVERSARY OF HIS DEATH
TORONTO

Void When Detached

The parking ticket
disclaimer
seems to sum up
my life.

&

*Time heals nothing.
It's not the passage of time,
it's what you do
with the time that counts.*

DR. PHIL MCGRAW

Struggling and Soaring with Angels

Frozen Emotions

I dream that I'm in my bedroom in Toronto. Standing at an east-facing window, I watch as black storm clouds roil rapidly toward me. As the gale reaches me, I see the wind whipping past the window, visible as wind when it slides at high velocity over an airplane wing. The wind turns to racing water, then snow, then ice. Then, most alarmingly, snow begins to amass *inside* the window sill. I run my hand along the sill and scoop up a snowball's worth of snow. Appalled, I show it to a friend, "Look. Snow *inside* the window. How am I going to survive here in the winter?"

What does this dream mean? I've moved away from a place where everyone so clearly saw my dead husband standing in the empty space beside me, to a place where I can start afresh. Starting afresh is good, but the price tag is high. I now have no support network of family and friends, my son is unhappy at his new school, and I feel "snowed under" at my new job.

I'm soldiering on, burying my emotions, trying to be super Mom, trying to do a great job at work, trying not to let anyone see how much this effort is costing me. I think this dream warns that if I allow my emotions to be frozen inside my own home, I will not survive. I will crack.

Aurora Winter

&

*I cannot give you the formula for success,
but I can give you the formula for failure,
which is: Try to please everybody.*

HERBERT BAYARD SWOPE

Struggling and Soaring with Angels

Divorce

I dream that I'm teaching a giggling four-year-old Yale to snorkel. I teach him how to hold his breath underwater. We swim and splash in a black, calm sea. Yale is great—he's practically a merboy! We're having fun.

David enters the dream. He's been vacationing with the guys.

I calmly ask him if he missed us. He says he forgot to miss us, forgot that we were a part of his life. I say it's just Yale and me now, always just the two of us, and we're doing fine. Matter-of-fact, I state that if he's always going to be taking vacations without us, and not even miss us, then we should get a divorce.

David concedes my point without a trace of rancor or hurt.

Now, David and I are walking on a dock floating on the calm, black, clear sea. Yale isn't there.

We dive into the black water together, holding hands, and swim underwater. Our destination is our home on another dock on the other side.

This dream reminds me of when we were in the Caribbean and I taught three-year-old Yale to swim while his father watched from the transom of the sailboat. Then, I had on flippers, and I felt like such a powerful swimmer, effortlessly able to keep myself afloat as well as guide Yale, who was also buoyed by a lifejacket. Except that on that day, the water was a clear, sparkling azure blue.

It's been almost four years since he died, but my subconscious mind still feels married. What is our home on

Aurora Winter

the dock on the other side? Will we be joined again once I cross over "to the other side"?

&

This existence of ours is as transient as autumn clouds.
To watch the birth and death of beings
is like looking at the movements of a dance.

BUDDHA

Struggling and Soaring with Angels

L.A.

The sun sets near Venice Beach. Magic hour. An impossibly slim and curvaceous blonde prances in the ocean, tossing her blonde tresses, swishing her thong-clad ass. Her orange bikini is bright against the gray waves. Why is she strutting?

Ahhh...a cameraman snaps photos, knee-deep in the rolling waves. His lens captures only the ocean and the beauty.

Behind him, there's a black derelict of a man, one leg gone at the thigh, the other gone at the knee. Dressed in dirty tatters, a crutch supporting him, he ventures as deep into the ocean as he can, as if—if he touched that impossibly perfect, glowing body—he would be made whole again.

The cameraman's lens captures only the light, shunning the gruesome shadow that lurks behind his back. Study in contrasts. Light and Dark. Life and Death. Welcome to Los Angeles.

&

*Romance and work are great diversions
to keep you from dealing with yourself.*

CHER

Aurora Winter

Dysfunctional Relationships

February—no, cross that out, November 15th. I'm so convinced that it's February. That's the fourth time today that I've been about to write "February" as the date. No wonder I feel leaden and depressed. February. Grief. Death.

I'm thinking that a great sexual relationship would distract me for a year or two, and a great sexual/friend relationship would probably distract me for a decade. And then? Then I'd feel the emptiness again. No wonder so many people "wake up" feeling empty after seven years. The relationship no longer distracts them from the emptiness within. So they blame the relationship—and move on to someone else—for another seven years.

Which is why people (yours truly) are sometimes attracted to dysfunctional relationships. The pain of sparring distracts our attention from a deeper, more inescapable pain within.

So the only answer is within. Finding balance within.

&

*Some people will never learn to understand anything
... because they understand everything too soon.*

ALEXANDER POPE

Struggling and Soaring with Angels

Another Dreary Christmas Looms

Yale and I walk along the beach. I'm in a cross, grumpy mood. I start crying. Christmas is coming, and it makes me miss David so much, miss being a "whole" family. Yale gives me a big hug and says, "It must be so much work to raise a kid all by yourself. And have a job, too. And I can't believe it, you are doing such a great job!"

I don't want my eight-year-old to have to be my emotional support. I reassure him that I'm not crying because it's so much work to look after him. He pipes up, "Yes, I'm very helpful. I unpack groceries and everything!"

I give him a big hug and tell him I'm just lonely, not overworked. I tell him that he's my joy and the light of my life, not a chore. He seems suitably reassured.

The sun glints off the waves like so many stars and seems to be trying to lick our feet. The great lakes are pretty, but polluted, so we don't play in the water.

I think it is still this sense of not working *toward* something, of just surviving, that is getting me down. David and I used to have so many plans for the future. So many dreams are now dust.

I'm tired, too. There is so much to do. I dread the weekends: taxes, bills, financial planning. It weighs heavily

Aurora Winter

on me, now that I must shoulder all the adult responsibilities in this family. Work seems lighter, more enjoyable than the weekends spent surrounded by responsibilities which are now mine alone.

&

In order to change, we must be sick and tired of being sick and tired.

ANONYMOUS

Struggling and Soaring with Angels

Caught by Surprise

At work, I saw a colleague wearing a dark brown Australian oilskin trench coat—just like the one David wore. Grief caught me suddenly at the throat. I gasped and had to stop a moment, collect myself, before proceeding into the meeting room.

&

Time does restore to us our quiet joy....
But all our lives we will be subject to sudden
small reminders which bring all the
old loss back overwhelmingly.

ELIZABETH WATSON

Aurora Winter

Partners in Love

David was so competent. He'd take any problem and make it go away. He was a good negotiator. I loved it that he was so assertive, like a German shepherd. He rarely worried, and he urged me to let my problems roll off me "like water off a duck's back." He'd say that all the time. I could trust him to navigate any seas, literal or figurative. We were quite a team. Together, it seemed we could do anything.

How I miss him. How I miss his wise counsel, his interest in my day, his love. How I miss his hands absent-mindedly stroking my feet as we'd watch TV (I felt like purring like a cat).

David, it's hard to remember the point of life without you. I love Yale so much, but everything seems like such a chore. Christmas looms like another thing on my "to do" list. I used to love Christmas so much. I'm trying to be happy. But it seems as though I don't have the energy to fight off this depression that keeps entangling me.

Struggling and Soaring with Angels

ॐ

Come to me, all you who are weary and burdened,
and I will give you rest.
Take my yoke upon you and learn from me,
for I am gentle and humble in heart,
and you will find rest for your souls.
For my yoke is easy and my burden is light.

JESUS, QUOTED IN MATTHEW 11:28-30

Aurora Winter

The Dog Died

After his father died, Yale barely seemed to grieve. At first, he hung to false hope. When that was crushed, he'd escape into the world of video games, or he'd cling to me. His childish crayon artwork was always of Yale and Mommy, as if to bind me tighter to him.

He lost his self-confidence and his Aries bravado and his certainty that the world was a safe place. (We both did).

I remember once when I left him, he wanted me to *promise* I'd be back. I told him that I loved him more than anything else in the world and that if I could come back, I most certainly would. But I couldn't promise. *(What if I'm hit by a truck?)* I couldn't give him an ironclad guarantee. Not honestly.

Sometimes he'd be sad, and his face would crumple. Sometimes he'd cry. At the beginning, he refused to enter anyone's home until he'd declared, "My dad is dead." Until that elephantine fact was acknowledged, he literally wouldn't cross the threshold.

At school, Father's Day hurt. So did some bedtime stories. But he didn't grieve deeply. He didn't have times of gut-wrenching inconsolable wailing—until the dog died.

Then, he wailed and sobbed as I rocked him on my lap. He talked about the dog—but it wasn't about the dog. It was about Death, about Loss, about his father. He was inconsolable.

By then, it was safe for him to grieve. He knew I was strong then, he felt safe to release his torrent of hot, sticky

Struggling and Soaring with Angels

emotions, as terrifying and horrific as they were. He knew I would hold him and rock him and console him.

He knew his hot tears wouldn't splash salt in my own raw wounds.

&

Love is patient, love is kind...
It always protects, always trusts,
always hopes, always perseveres.
Love never fails.

1 CORINTHIANS 13:4, 7–8

Aurora Winter

Mother's Magic

I am so angry! I'm furious that I have to do everything all by myself. I'm irate that I never have time alone. I'm upset that I can't pay bills or play the piano for five minutes without interruption. I'm angry that when I'm angry I have to be so calm and rational and reasonable and listen first and not slam doors or cry or pout or upset my role as the Good Mom.

I try to be a Good Mom, but I've lost my mother's magic. My hugs, which used to make everything okay, can't do that anymore. I can't make everything all better for Yale. I can't bring his father back. I can't heal his tender heart. My impotence infuriates me.

I have to vent my feelings or I am going to explode. Even though there is no one to listen but God.

&

Just as a snake sheds its skin,
we must shed our past—over and over again.

BUDDHA

Struggling and Soaring with Angels

I'm a Little Spider

We play "I'm a little teapot" on the piano. Yale makes up this song:

"I'm a little spider with my web—don't get caught, or I'll be fed. If you're very juicy, that'll be good—just don't barf, or I won't feel good. I'm a little spider with my web—don't get caught, or you'll be dead!"

We giggle and clown around. Yale teaches his song to me, and we sing it together. Yale is so cute I could just eat him up!

&

Wake up with a smile and go after life....
Live it, enjoy it, taste it, smell it, feel it.

JOE KNAPP

Aurora Winter

A Widower

It's almost four years to the day that he died. I feel like a raw wound. As in *Iron John*, is my wound that which turns to gold? I sure hope so. If only all this pain could serve some purpose, then it would be bearable.

I talk to Paul (a writer I haven't met yet) to reschedule our lunch meeting. I propose breakfast, and he says no, then quickly changes it to yes. Laughing, he says, "My wife taught me that the only appropriate answer when a woman wants something is those three magic words: I'll be there."

I laugh, saying that, with an attitude like that, he must have a great marriage. There's a pause, then he says his wife died five years ago of breast cancer.

My breath clogs in my throat, and I cannot speak.

He goes on and on, talking easily, joking about how he raised her two kids from a previous marriage through those teenaged years. (Her daughter saying, "Hi, this is Spike, and I love him, and I'm *going* to have sex with him whether you give me birth control or not.") Her two kids are grown and have left home now. It's another beginning for him.

Finally, I'm able to loosen my throat enough to share that I'm a widow.

He's surprised. He's thirty-nine, and he's never met a young widow. We have something in common. He starts afresh and says how people, learning of his wife's cancer upon meeting her, would say things like, "Oh! I had an uncle who died of cancer last year." Trying to establish common ground—but unintentionally hurting.

Struggling and Soaring with Angels

209

He understood why I have not opened all those condolence cards. Same thing. He understood the drama of tragedy, the longing not to be "The Aurora Winter Show!"

I talk little. He talks honestly and freely. I hang up and sob. Deep, wrenching grief. I leave early and start crying again as I drive home.

Yale asks me, "How was your day?"

"I had a sad day," I confess.

"Why?"

"I was missing Dad."

"Don't make me sad," Yale says, and leaves abruptly.

That's uncharacteristic. Usually, he'd give me a hug or try to cheer me up. He must be hurting, too. He must know that it is almost the anniversary of his father's death, even though we haven't talked about it.

In the morning, when Yale wakes up, he has a nosebleed.

&

There is an alchemy in sorrow.
It can be transmuted into wisdom,
which, if it does not bring joy,
can yet bring happiness.

PEARL S. BUCK

Fourth Anniversary

Four years pass. A new friend observes that I have the quality of an open wound.

I no longer live in the house he built. I've moved 3,000 miles from the life we shared. Our son is twice as old now, half his life he's spent without a father.

Four years to the day. My son and I skate on the Rideau Canal with some old friends.

A heaviness sits on my chest, crushing me, suffocating me. There's a dead man on my chest. If I pushed his dead body off me—I could skate, I could fly, I could dance.

But I cannot shrug off his weight. I will not let him crumple onto the cold, hard ice.

I loved this man.

&

*Death ends a life,
not a relationship.*

MORRIE SCHWARTZ

Struggling and Soaring with Angels

211

Cannes TV Festival

I love my life. Here I am in the south of France at the Cannes Television Festival. Television producers, distributors, and broadcasters converge from all over the world to schmooze and make deals. Everyone looks fabulous, and the setting is breathtaking. The Mediterranean Sea is a glorious azure blue, the beaches are white sand, the food is exquisite.

I meet the most amazing British producer at a meeting, "Nigel." Later, he takes me out for drinks and dinner. He shares that when our knees accidentally bumped under the table at the meeting, he felt a jolt of electricity and realized he had to get to know me better.

He seems amazing. Maybe he's the one.

&

*It is the nature of grace to always fill
spaces that have been empty.*

GOETHE

Aurora Winter

International Film and TV Production

I leave Toronto and Atlantis and move to Newport Beach, California to start a film and television production company with Nigel. I'm completely, madly, deeply in love and tell my father (and anyone else who will listen) that I'm going to marry Nigel. Nigel completes me—he's the one.

Nigel remains in London so that we can set up European co-productions, and one of my old friends from Atlantis, Tom, becomes our Canadian collaborator, so that we can also do Canadian-content productions. It seems a brilliant plan with so many benefits: Canadian content, European content, and even an office in California near the world's entertainment capital, Hollywood.

I live in a small home with a stunning view of Newport Harbor. The rent is outrageously expensive, and so is my new BMW, but it doesn't matter. In the film business, appearances are everything. Besides, soon we're going to be incredibly successful.

&

Strong hope is a much greater stimulant of life than any single realized joy could be.

FRIEDERICH NIETZSCHE

Struggling and Soaring with Angels

Going to Church

I don't think I've ever worked so hard for so long and had so little to show for it. I started going to Mariner's Church regularly. The minister, Kenton Beshore, is a very gifted orator.

The music is lovely, but I almost always cry. I feel so unworthy. I feel like such a failure. Nothing seems to be working out quite as I had planned. I don't know what else to do, except try harder—and pray.

&

The value of consistent prayer is not
that He will hear us,
but that we will hear Him.

WILLIAM MCGILL

Aurora Winter

Dream: College Pastor

I dream that I'm going to college. I'm new, sad, and lonely. I see a young pastor in a little welcome booth inside a college building. He smiles and catches my eye. I continue on my way, but then decide—he looked friendly, I could be bold and talk to him. What have I got to lose? But first, I need to park.

There's snow on the ground everywhere, and I have a great deal of difficulty parking because every open parking space is chained off limits. In the dream, my car turns into a mere bicycle which I ride through the snow. I still can't find a place to park, but decide I can just wheel the bike inside the building.

This obstacle overcome, I return to the building. But now the friendly young pastor has disappeared from the church welcome booth. An old priest is there, but he doesn't look approachable, and he's busy talking to a group of people. Disappointed, I turn away.

Then I realize that the church is hosting a casual welcome in a nearby classroom. I pluck up my courage and enter the classroom. Late, I disrupt the group. The friendly young pastor graciously seats me, saying that everyone's just been introducing themselves. He asks me a question or two, giving me the opportunity to reveal myself to the group.

I respond brilliantly, smoothly—too smoothly. I reveal none of my pain, none of my searching, none of my soul. I could be a politician making a televised campaign speech.

Struggling and Soaring with Angels

The pastor sees through my façade. "What if you had only forty days to live?"

The question is so profound, so challenging, so God-given, I wake up with a gasp.

&

Get real.

DR. PHIL MCGRAW

Long Distance Romance

My phone bill is almost $2,000 this month. This long-distance romance is wearing thin. I love the business, but am tired of being only business partners. I want to get married. Nigel wants to be successful first. I want him to move to California and live with me. He wants to stay in England and visit frequently.

Our production company is based upon a brilliant plan, except for one "minor" oversight. The situation reminds me of an invading fleet in a science fiction book by Douglas Adams. Prepared for battle and for victory, the alien force materializes out of hyperspace, ready to take over planet Earth. But, due to a slight miscalculation of scale, the entire invading armada is swallowed by a small dog.

Our company is grossly understaffed and underfinanced. Hollywood swallows us as a Great Dane might inhale a flea. Barely even noticing.

We've enjoyed some success. A movie and TV series I created are developed by broadcasters, resulting in modest cash injections. But it's not enough to offset our overhead, flights from L.A. to London, and trips to the Cannes Television Festival. In fact, it's not even enough to cover my annual phone bill.

The financial strain is taking its toll on our relationship and our business. Nigel's savings have been used up, and he's now borrowing money from his mother. I'm growing increasingly resentful of the fact that I'm bearing the brunt of the financial burden of operating this company.

Struggling and Soaring with Angels

My girlfriend Bonnie visits from Whistler. Meeting Nigel, she comments that he looks a lot like David. Funny—that never occurred to me before. But now that she has pointed it out, I realize the resemblance is striking.

I think long and hard. Do I really love him? Or did I just think I could recapture what I had lost? There are so many similarities. Nigel looks like David, has big dreams like David, and we're in business together, like I was with David.

I have to face the fact that David isn't coming back. Not in any form, not in any way, not in any person. I will never have my old life back. *Never.*

I lost a lot of money, but regained pieces of my scattered self. I remembered who I was—who I *am*. Even without David, I can write a business plan, forecast financials, solve problems, market, sell, follow up, and close a deal. I'm good in a pitch meeting, and I'm a good writer. I'm capable. I'm not a pathetic widow who needs charity and needs someone to look after her. Not that Nigel is looking after me. It's more the other way around.

Nigel isn't David. David would never be such a financial burden to a business partner. Or a girlfriend.

With a heavy heart, I decide to move on, although our business is on the cusp of raising several million dollars in funding in London. I give up my share of the business and the first man I deeply loved since my husband died.

Yale is wretched, too. Nigel made him laugh. He used to make us both laugh.

Aurora Winter

218

Forgiveness means letting go of the past.

GERALD JAMPOLSKY

Struggling and Soaring with Angels

Finding a Job

Now, I *really* need a job. I don't have much experience job hunting. I've been self-employed most of my life, in business with my husband or Nigel. A friend who works at Disney, Lee, knows of a job opening at a small film and television company based in Los Angeles. Lee suggests that I go to the TV festival in New Orleans and meet with Bruce, the President of PorchLight Entertainment. Lee puts in a good word on my behalf, and I secure a meeting with Bruce.

While I'm waiting for my scheduled appointment, I wander around the television convention. A woman recognizes me and gushes about how much she loved *Dragon Claws*—the very first screenplay I was paid to write. She was on the adjudicating committee that awarded it funding over a hundred other applicants. I'd almost forgotten my first paid gig. Being affirmed by this stranger is just the energy I need. A far better pick-me-up than a coffee.

I meet Bruce and pitch a series I created that is in development with a Canadian broadcaster. We hit it off, and he invites me to continue the discussion over drinks. Unlike my meeting with Seaton, this time I know that he has a job opening, and this time I'm positioning myself for an offer.

By the end of the evening, he hints that he might have an employment opportunity for me. It takes a few months and a few meetings to close the deal, but once again I land a prestigious job with a lucrative salary. This time, I know what I'm worth, and I negotiate hard to get the figure I

Aurora Winter

know he'll pay and the film and television credits I know I'll earn.

The only catch is, now I have to move, uproot us both once again and move closer to Los Angeles. I decide that it's a small price to pay for employment with PorchLight Entertainment as the Vice President of Development and Production.

&

*Life is like a game of cards.
The hand that is dealt you represents determinism;
the way you play it is free will.*

NEHRU

Producing Movies

I work on a number of interesting television and film projects. My first movie is a co-production with Mind's Eye Pictures—the same company that produced *Eli's Lesson*. Small world.

This time, when I go to Regina, I'm not going as a lowly writer, but as the executive representing the U.S. partner, PorchLight, and U.S. broadcaster, Showtime. *Stranger in Town* is a well-written script by John Hopkins. I meet Harry Hamlin and other members of the cast and crew, including the director, Stuart Margolin.

Back in L.A., I watch cut after cut of the movie. I'm amazed by how the same footage can be edited into such shockingly different versions of the same story, some garbled and incomprehensible, others over-simplified. It's a mystery, so planting the clues with a skillful touch, neither too light nor too heavy-handed, requires great editing.

I'm thrilled to have the opportunity to set up *The Screwtape Letters* by one of my favorite authors, C. S. Lewis, which is "in turnaround" from a major studio. I approach John Cleese to star, but he passes. In the end, I'm unable to get this project off the ground, due to complications with the producer attached to it who insists on directing in spite of his lack of experience. Most projects—even good ones—never make it out of "development hell" and into production. There is too much competition, too many things to go wrong, and too much money involved.

One project that does get produced is *Treehouse Hostage*, a feature film which stars Jim Varney (better known as

Ernest). The director, Sean McNamara, has a great eye. He casts brilliantly and does wonders stretching his modest budget. This movie is a winning kid-pleaser, and I'm delighted to be credited as co-executive producer.

&

To love what you do and feel that it matters—
how could anything be more fun?

KATHERINE GRAHAM

Struggling and Soaring with Angels

My Mom

By: Yale Winter, age 13

My Mom is no ordinary person. She has helped me through hard times and taught me things like no one else could. My Mom has blue eyes and blonde hair and likes to ski a lot. My Mom is such a fabulous Mom and friend to me.

I admire the way my Mom runs her life. She's always got some kind of schedule to keep. How she is always asking me if I need help with my homework, and still letting me do a lot of things that other kids don't get to do. I like how she chooses to ask me whether I want to go see a movie or go out to eat somewhere or something.

My Mom makes my life very worthwhile and gives me a great day every day and all days. With my Mom, every day is different even though it's almost the same. My Mom finds some way to make basically everything more exciting. I think that my Mom feels the same way about her life (except when she has to pay the bills) she seems to be living a worthwhile life.

My Mom does so many things every day that help me one way or another. It's not like she saved my life once, but more like she does smaller things all the time. My Mom has always been really honest to me. She never lies or makes light of things to me. Like when my Dad passed away, my Mom told me the truth. I really appreciate that she did and didn't lie because if she did, that probably would have made it harder later on.

Aurora Winter

My Mom totally makes every second of every day in my life totally worthwhile. Without my Mom I would be lost in the big maze of life. I hope my Mom and me continue to be such good friends.

&

Rather than love, than money,
than fame, give me truth.

HENRY DAVID THOREAU

Coming Full Circle

I leave PorchLight Entertainment and focus on my writing career. I'd really like to crack the episodic market. To date, all my writing has been original, but I'm told I need to generate some writing samples for existing TV series. I take a course in episodic writing and write a spec *Buffy the Vampire Slayer* script. I get an "A" from my UCLA instructor. Thinking I need to show more range (most of my screenplays are family or fantasy), I also write a *Law & Order: Special Victims Unit* spec script.

I take pitch meeting after pitch meeting. Things seem encouraging—but "encouraging" doesn't pay the rent. Too often, in the end, executives are more interested in dating me than hiring me. Another TV series I wrote and created stirs up a lot of interest at Paramount, but I don't receive the promised paperwork or option fee, in spite of help from Stu at William Morris.

I love writing, but my bank account is looking sickly. At this rate, I won't be sending my son to college—and that's unacceptable. I realize I have a much bigger financial opportunity—it's just not writing, and it's not in Los Angeles.

Many times, I'd toyed with the idea of selling the house that David built in Whistler. And now I'm so glad that I listened to Bonnie's wise counsel and didn't. Real estate values in Whistler have skyrocketed. David's predictions about property values came true. Not that I would have been able to sell our dream house—before this, anyway. I had so many emotions tangled up in it.

Aurora Winter

My Mother encourages me to sell that house and stop living in rented places in California. That makes sense. My older brother Calvin has been incredibly supportive and has looked after my house during my absences. He concurs. It would be a good time to sell.

Now, I can justify finishing the house. I'm so glad I didn't invest the money earlier, when the value would have been eroded by time and renters. Now I can put proper light fixtures where there are bare bulbs. I can put a proper floor where there is painted concrete. I can stop feeling ashamed of the way the house is finished; stop feeling that I have to explain why such a big house on such a stunning lakefront lot is so barren inside. The parallels between the house and my own life are eerie and unmistakable.

I review the real estate market in Whistler and realize that high-end homes are selling for a premium. A more extensive renovation would reap the greatest rewards. Over the years, large, luxurious homes owned by the "rich and famous" have gradually displaced small cabins owned by locals. For instance, my immediate neighbor was once a Whistler realtor, but is now an Academy Award winning screenwriter, Eric Roth. He won an Oscar for writing the screenplay for *Forrest Gump* which starred Tom Hanks and, more recently, wrote *The Insider* which starred Russell Crowe.

While I suffer a great deal of emotional turmoil making decisions about this property and spin my wheels in "analysis paralysis," eventually I hire my brother Bryce to be my interior designer, obtain the financing required for the renovation, interview general contractors, and review and approve the plans and budget. I'm still anxious about the amount of money I'm spending. I agonize endlessly

Struggling and Soaring with Angels

227

over decisions. I fret that the plans Bryce cajoles me into approving, which look good on paper, won't work in reality.

I call my friend Brahm, and he listens with seemingly inexhaustible patience as I go over and over (and over and over) each tortured decision. (Later, I realize that all this churning in my mind was a way of avoiding, at least for a moment, the real work which was being done, which was the work of grieving, the work of letting go, and I forgive myself for being so indecisive, dense and obsessive.)

Finally, on Valentine's Day, a few days before the ninth anniversary of David's death, I take the plunge. I hire the general contractor and give the renovation the "green light."

Five months later, when the renovation is complete, I am euphoric. The house is so beautiful, I could cry for sheer joy. David would be so proud. It's not a Shattered Dream House any more. It is *my* stunning house. It has solid marble and limestone countertops, a kitchen sparkling with commercial-style stainless steel appliances and custom solid wood cabinets, a huge hot tub, and a spectacular view of Whistler and Blackcomb ski hills and Alta Lake. The bare concrete floor has been replaced with beautiful pine and slate floors. It even has real light fixtures—no more bare bulbs. The house is transformed. And so am I.

Selling this home will provide one final gift from my husband: a college education and more secure future for my son. No, that's not right. The gift is not only from my husband. With a lot of help from my friends and family, this gift for my son is from me, too.

In spite of Yale's protests about leaving his friends in California, I decide that we need to live full time in this house in Whistler. I tell myself I'll enhance the value of

Aurora Winter

228

the home by being there. But the truth is, I need to go back, I need to come full circle.

&

We are very near to greatness:
one step and we are safe;
can we not take the leap?

RALPH WALDO EMERSON

Struggling and Soaring with Angels

Final Occupancy

I received the final occupancy permit for the house today. What a sweet triumph. All the little outstanding things on the house have been completed and officially stamped as "approved." I feel my own sense of completion, my own sense of being approved.

David would be pleased. And so am I.

&

If at first you don't succeed, try, try, try again.

W. E. HICKSON

Aurora Winter

Valentine's Day

Almost ten years have passed since the day he died. In just five days, the length of time I've been grieving will be the length of time we shared.

I review my life and ruefully realize that I've been running (bolting, some have said) racing, hurling myself forward so as to avoid looking back.

Yet, like a cat's tail, my past chases me. It's only now that I've had the strength to come full circle and return to the beginning. Return to our broken dreams, the house my husband built with such love, yet never lived in.

It's only now that I've gone through boxes and boxes of his clothes and photos and little things. Can you believe it?

I deserve some kind of award for procrastination. This letting go has taken so many tries, so many phases, and in my defense, I've let go of many things before this. But then, I couldn't bear to part with any more. I couldn't bear to let go of the lingering trace of his scent on an old frayed tee shirt.

So I put everything in boxes and left it all behind in our Dream House—our Shattered Dream House.

Until now. After almost a decade of running away, I've come back home. Bit by bit, I've faced the mountain of memories. Sometimes I had to repeat the mantra, *He's not this tee shirt, he's not this chair*, to coax my fingers to loosen their grip, to coax my heart to let go.

I gave away the mattress he died on. Can you believe I still had that? I just couldn't deal with it before. Waves of

Struggling and Soaring with Angels

raw grief hit me as I faced that mattress and relived his death anew, as though it had been yesterday. And I sobbed inconsolably.

This grieving business is such hard work. When my husband died, I thought I'd be better in a year. But it has been almost ten years, and I know I'm not better. I'm a sprinter by nature so it has been hard to endure this marathon of grieving.

In anticipation of yet another anniversary, I review this decade of grief, of burying myself in work, of stealing comfort from "boys" brave enough—or foolish enough—to compete with a ghost, of moving almost every year, of being unable to make long-term plans.

I don't like what I see. I want to get better. I want to be whole again. In *Mars and Venus on a Date*, Dr. John Gray states that, until we have an open heart, we're doomed to repeat our patterns.

I close the book and pray earnestly to God. I pray for an open heart. I pray for healing. It's the day before Valentine's Day.

The next morning, Bonnie calls me. She has a treat for me for Valentine's Day. It's a massage because she knows my back has been bothering me. Bonnie insists that I receive her gift, so I go to see Joy.

I tell Joy where my back hurts (at the bra strap), and she tells me that that's my heart chakra. Then she reveals that she's trained in very specialized energy work called *Sekhem*, that opens the heart. Am I open to that?

I laugh as grateful tears well up. When I prayed for an open heart, I didn't expect God to move so quickly!

Aurora Winter

Joy works on me, her hands barely touching me. I will myself to heal, I ask God for an open heart. But my body is stiff and unyielding.

She guides me through a meditation. I'm drifting down a stream floating on my back on a lily pad. Cherub-like child-me finds everything delightful, is completely entranced by the wonder of my own fingers, laughs with delight at the fluttering butterflies, chortles with mirth as leaves release from trees and dance to the stream below.

I'm nestled in my own rich imagination. When Joy begins to move the energy around my heart chakra, I see a yellow bud. It is gradually opening. A second later, she tells me I'll see a yellow flower opening. But I've already seen it.

The yellow rose opens, its petals are tipped with red. Again, she paints this picture for me, describing my vision in instant replay. My mind finds this intriguing.

Then she tells me that she sees my husband in the room, that he's here with us now. He gives me a dozen red roses and lays them on my chest. They're so real I can feel the weight of them, I can almost catch their fragrance. Tears well up.

She tells me David loves me. He wants to take my burdens and carry them. He wants me to give him my burdens now. She tells me it's safe to let go. Deep sobs shake my body and hot tears stream down my face. She tells me I can give him my burdens any time. He wants to carry them. He's always with me.

I feel a heaviness leave my body. I feel a deep release, as though a lead knot in my heart evaporated.

Later, when she has finished, she thanks *me* for the experience! She says she has only experienced pure bliss twice in her life, and this was the second time. When she

Struggling and Soaring with Angels

felt the love pouring from my husband to me, it was channeled through her, and she was filled with love, a love so pure it transported her to bliss.

She tells me that, whenever I feel anxious or fearful, it is because I don't have an open heart. Then I need to take a quiet moment, see my yellow rose, and know that I am loved and I am loving, and choose to have an open heart. Love is the key.

&

The highest power is to act, feel and think from an open heart. When our hearts are open, we are able to act in accordance with our highest purpose, which is to love.

DR. JOHN GRAY

Aurora Winter

Inspiration: C. S. Lewis

I'm going to write a book to help others through grief. If I can make even one person's journey a little easier, a little more certain, it'll be worth the effort. I feel so thankful to be finally through my own dark tunnel of grief. This book will be my "thank you," my way of giving back to all those who helped me through the dark days: friends, family, and strangers who reached out to me through the written word.

I've always wanted to write a book. Actually, I did write a science fiction novel before I got swept up in the film business. I just didn't show it to anyone besides David.

I've been toying with ideas for a kid's book, like *The Lion, the Witch and the Wardrobe* by my hero, C. S. Lewis. I still remember where the Narnian series of books were shelved in the elementary school library and the mixture of anticipation and awe I would feel as I took each book from the shelf. As my eager fingers slipped around each precious volume, I was practically transported into Narnia. I remember feeling bereft when I had read them all. Those books planted my dream of being a writer. A great writer like C. S. Lewis.

But C. S. Lewis wrote another book that touched me deeply, *A Grief Observed*. He shared his journal of grieving after his wife died. Even though his circumstances were very different from mine, reading his ranting soothed me profoundly, gave me hope, and made me feel that I was not alone. Others had gone into the darkness of grief and survived.

Struggling and Soaring with Angels

I'm going to follow in my hero's footsteps and share my own journals of grieving and healing. I know that compiling the material from my volumes of journals will be cathartic for me. I feel compelled to write the book I wished I could have read when I was grieving. A book filled with the conversations and quotes I'd share with my dearest friend if she was struggling with grief.

&

This is the true joy in life: The being used for a purpose
recognized by yourself as a mighty one.
The being a force of nature, instead of a feverish,
selfish little clod of ailments and grievances complaining
that the world will not devote itself to making you happy.
I am of the opinion that my life belongs to the whole community,
and as long as I live, it is my privilege to do for it whatever I can.

GEORGE BERNARD SHAW

Aurora Winter

Prayer

Rereading my journals, I see how gradually God has cultivated in me a daily habit of prayer. What used to be simply a time of writing in my journal has slowly but surely expanded to include meditation or silent reflection, inspirational reading or bible study, affirmations or prayer. Writing, reading, meditating, and prayer all helped me work through grief and gradually come to terms with the truth.

As I reread my journals, I have a new sense of time. Life is long.

I'm also moved to see how many prayers have been answered. Many times, by the time my prayer was answered, I had forgotten that I had even prayed for it. Therefore, I failed to be properly grateful for my answered prayers.

When David died, I never thought we'd survive. But it has been ten years, and God has faithfully provided for us all this time. God does provide. One day at a time.

❧

There are seasons of prayer which,
though spent amid distractions
and tediousness, are yet,
owing to a good intention,
fruitful to the heart.

FRANÇOIS DE SALIGNAC DE LA MOTHE FÉNELON

Struggling and Soaring with Angels

Spreading His Ashes

It's been ten years. I've carried my husband's ashes from North Vancouver to Whistler to Toronto to Newport Beach to Santa Monica to Whistler once again. The ashes and I have come full circle.

And now it feels like time to let his ashes go. To set him free. To set myself free.

I talk to Yale about it, and he says, "Didn't we already do that?"

He has no pangs or hang-ups, no fear of letting go. I admire his simple, unstrained approach. As we get older, we don't get wiser. We get gnarled and knotted.

I think a simple ceremony with just the two of us spreading David's ashes into Alta Lake (a pristine mountain lake beside the house he built) would be perfect. I resolve to do that on his birthday, June 28th, when the ice will have melted and the lake will be warm and full of laughter.

His ashes will flow from this lake he loved, down the River of Golden Dreams (how aptly named) and into the ocean he loved to sail. It seems idyllic, peaceful, and serene.

But, as the ice melts on the lake and winter gives way to spring, I realize that, while I lost a husband, and my son lost his father, others lost a son, a brother.

The last time we grieved together it was a disaster. I narrowly escaped being permanently shunned by my in-laws (Yale alone saved me). So I dread the thought of spreading his ashes together, knowing how easy it is for tortuous grief to be displaced by simple anger—and that I'm the lightening rod. But I want to do the right thing.

Aurora Winter

238

I talk to his parents. They cry and share they've often wondered what I had done with his ashes (though they never breathed a word to me). It seems an incredible relief to them that I want to honor their wishes and include them. I even offer to give them the ashes, but they don't want them. Don't even want to see the urn.

They're very supportive and agree that it's time. We agree to do it this summer and to give more thought to where.

Afterwards, my stomach is knotted with emotion, but I know I did the right thing. *Honor thy father and thy mother.* And surrender.

&

There is within each of us a potential for goodness beyond our imagining: for giving which seeks no reward; for listening without judgment; for loving unconditionally.

ELIZABETH KUBLER-ROSS

My Father-in-Law's 70th Birthday

Thirty people have gathered from across Canada to pay tribute to my father-in-law, Don, and his wife, Doreen. The party is held at the yacht club in Gibsons. I am deeply moved to hear story after story from friends and employees whose lives he profoundly touched.

A lady named Linda stands up, compelled to acknowledge my father-in-law, as her husband Darwin squirms in his chair. They're now in their twilight years, but she talks about when they were just married and broke. As President of Barber-Ellis Paper, my father-in-law gave Darwin a much-needed job. But Darwin barely had time to learn the names of his coworkers before he fell ill. Weeks slipped by, and Darwin's health was still faltering. Linda told Don that she didn't know when her husband would be able to return to work. Or even *if* he would be able to return. Instead of platitudes, my father-in-law reassured her that Darwin's job would be waiting for him, no matter how long it took. Linda's voice shakes with emotion, and grateful tears run down her cheeks. There's no doubt in her mind that my father-in-law changed the entire course of their lives for the better.

Dad honors me by asking me to be a speaker. Gerard, the eldest son, leads us in prayer, while the youngest son, Mike, is funny and irreverent. And now, it is my turn. All eyes turn expectantly towards me. I know I'm not just speaking for me. I am the voice of the missing son.

Aurora Winter

I speak from the heart. "Dad has taught me the meaning of family. He has modeled steadfast commitment to family—no matter what. Family is about always being there when it counts. I can honestly say that Dad has seen me at my darkest hour and at my finest hour, and he has been unfailingly supportive throughout."

Words flow easily. I conclude my tribute with heart-felt gratitude. "I am honored and blessed to be part of this family. I want to thank Dad—and Mom—for welcoming me into this family and for giving me such a great husband—and such a great son."

Dad is not the only one overcome with emotion. I take my seat, appreciating that I honored him—and David—effectively.

The supreme gift of this celebration is that I realize that it was not some lucky fluke that David was my husband. We were a good match.

&

The only gift is a portion of thyself.
Thou must bleed for me....
We can receive anything from love.

RALPH WALDO EMERSON

Struggling and Soaring with Angels

His Birthday, Forgiveness, and Farewell

Today is David's birthday. If he were alive, he'd be forty-four. It's pouring. For some reason, I thought it would be sunny on his birthday. It was so sunny the day he died.

I had hoped to spread his ashes on the lake today. But his parents want to be present and want David's brothers and their families to be present, and they don't feel ready. Remembering the last horrific time we celebrated David's birthday together, I suggest that Yale and I could spread a few of David's ashes today, leaving the rest for his family to spread whenever and wherever they see fit. But that compromise is unacceptable.

Yale and I are returning to California in two weeks. I'm not going to take David's ashes with me. I've carried them with me for ten years. That's long enough.

I've spent this year in Whistler facing my grief, my shattered dreams, my boxed-up feelings, and I *really* wanted to spread his ashes to symbolize the completion of that process. Oh, well. I have to let go of that. I've had ten years to get to the place where it would feel all right to let go. His family can take as long as they need. My father-in-law continues to teach me about the meaning of family, and I realize that it is most meaningful to honor his wishes.

My father-in-law has respected my desire not to take the ashes with me and has agreed to keep the urn.

I want to let go of David while I'm still here in Whistler, still here in this house he built. This has been a

Aurora Winter

242

year of accepting his death and releasing my knotted-up feelings. Now, I want to release him. Once and for all.

But David isn't his ashes. I can do this with a prayer and by releasing—not his ashes—but of the part of *me* that's been holding on to him, holding on to this house, holding on to the dreams it represented, even though they were stillborn, even holding on to my guilt and sorrow. I need to release it all. Gently release it *all*.

Seeking guidance and inspiration, I flip open the Bible and it opens at Ecclesiastes 3. It's perfect. My voice chokes with emotion as I read it.

> *There is a time for everything,*
> *And a season for every activity under heaven:*
> *A time to be born and a time to die,*
> *A time to plant and a time to uproot,*
> *A time to kill and a time to heal,*
> *A time to tear down and a time to build,*
> *A time to weep and a time to laugh,*
> *A time to mourn and a time to dance.*

ECCLESIASTES 3 V 1–4

I release all my grief, all my guilt, all my regrets, all my broken dreams. I ask David and God for forgiveness. I forgive myself. I forgive David for dying. I forgive God for taking him from us.

My voice is thick with emotion, and I pray at length, tears flowing. Before lighting the candle, I meditate quietly. Listening for guidance, I ask if any important words have been left unspoken. It is essential that this ceremony is

Struggling and Soaring with Angels

243

final, that everything is said. But I hear no prompting. I tell God He knows my heart and, if I have left anything unspoken, to speak those words for me. I invoke the most powerful prayer I know and bind up all my feelings of grief, guilt, shame, regret, anger etc. in the blood of Jesus Christ and banish Satan from my prayers and from my life. And I pray for God to use me for a worthy cause.

In the name of the Father, the Son, and the Holy Ghost, I light my symbolic candle, claiming the moment of alchemy as my own. I pray that both the dead wick and I be transformed to a living light.

I feel complete—and transformed.

&

When I have forgiven myself
and remembered who I am,
I will bless everyone and everything I see.

A COURSE IN MIRACLES

Aurora Winter

The Sweetest Triumph

We've moved again. But this time, it's different. I'm not running away. I've moved for my son, so that he can be with his best friend, so that he can go to the best school, so that he can have the best opportunities. For the first time, I've made a commitment to stay put for at least three years so that he can have the stability he needs to flourish.

Yale is fifteen now and in grade ten. Since he was seven, he has wanted to be a computer game designer. I'm in awe of what he has already achieved. He has designed many 2-D games and posted them on his own web page. He has mastered several programs, each time pushing the software to its limits and beyond. He has a mentor, Tarrnie, who works at Electronic Arts and who makes time to challenge Yale each week. Each week, Yale accepts the challenge and designs and builds more and more elaborate 3-D games.

Yale is the only fifteen-year-old at his school to get the special permission required to take Digital Arts 2. Even though his classmates are two years older, even though he didn't take Digital Arts 1, even though he's not familiar with Macs, I knew he'd shine. At the school's open house, it is Yale's work, and his alone, that is shown as a sample of class work.

Yale has been at his new school for three weeks. Over dinner, he shares his day. "You should see Sarah's house. It's huge! And Mikee has *two* huge houses. Our place is so small. And everyone has cell phones, too, Mom."

"Try not to get caught up in it, honey. Newport Beach is a very affluent area."

Struggling and Soaring with Angels

"I feel like the Sina of Newport Beach."

"What do you mean?"

"You know, how he had the smallest house, but everyone went there anyway, because he's so sociable."

"That's great that you have so many friends already. Anyway, we can't afford a bigger place. This is a good townhouse and big enough for just the two of us."

"Yeah, it's a good house," he says wistfully, not wanting to hurt my feelings.

I tell him about my day of writing and share that, as soon as I finish this book, I'm going to get a job.

"Your life would be so much easier if you had a husband."

"That's true," I agree, without even a trace of bitterness.

"Then you could just concentrate on your book or just concentrate on making money and not have to do both."

"True."

Yale wants to know more about this book. For the first time, I read him parts of it, sharing some things he said when he was five and the time that he touched Daddy's ashes. He laughs and says, "I remember that!" Then he gets serious and asks, "Was it hard? Raising me all by yourself?"

"Yes, sometimes."

He looks sad.

"But you saved my life," I explain. "Because I loved you and you loved me, it gave me direction and the will to go on. You gave my life meaning and purpose. You still do."

Yale reflects on this. "You know, you really are the best mom in the whole world."

I smile, but don't really absorb the compliment.

Aurora Winter

He insists, "No, really. My friends may have bigger houses, but I honestly don't know any other kid whose mom takes them as seriously and really supports their dreams. I mean, you bought me a great new computer and software and web hosting. And you drive me to L.A. to see Tarrnie."

I beam as my son affirms how rich his life is. He's only fifteen, but already he's wise, kind, loving, sensitive, caring, curious, driven, dedicated, goal-oriented, persistent, passionate, and perceptive. He's a good kid. No, he's a *great* kid.

My role in helping him become all he can be is the sweetest triumph of all.

&

Happy Mother's Day
To: the greatest Mom ever

Your excellence is unsurpassed
And no obstacle stands in your path.
You raised me as a child
And you still teach me, though I'm wild.
You're the greatest Mom ever
And you're always my Mom forever.

YALE WINTER, AGE 16

Struggling and Soaring with Angels

Cause of Death

The penny drops. How could I carry so much guilt for my husband's death for a decade, feeling I had somehow caused his demise, when the real culprit is so obvious? Why did it take me until now to identify the cause of his death? What is it about grieving that so distorts focus? Events immediately surrounding death assume such disproportionate importance, while earlier, pivotal events fade into a blurry background. They disappear, as a bird on a tree outside would disappear if you were trying to see it through a microscope.

About six months before his death, while David was building our house, he had concrete poured for the foundation from a huge cement-mixer. He warned the crusty old truck driver to make sure that the metal arm from the cement-mixer didn't hit the power lines. But the old guy just grumbled. He didn't need some young upstart to tell him his business.

Inside the metal arm was a rubber sleeve. David held this rubber tube, directing the stream of cement into the forms for the foundation. But the old guy got careless, and the metal arm touched the overhead power lines. The air cracked like thunder. A lethal surge of electricity arced like lightening from the power line to the truck's metal arm. The incredible blast felled David and threw the old man to the ground.

Five miles away, I heard the boom. The accident took out the power for half the town.

Aurora Winter

248

David seemed to be okay, just shaken up. Had he been holding the metal arm rather than the rubber sleeve inside it, he would certainly have been killed.

Later, buoyed by youth's unshakable sense of invincibility, we laughed about the incident. After all, I was only thirty, and he was only thirty-two. But a few months later, his arms started to go numb when he was sleeping. I insisted that he see a doctor. The doctor said it was nothing to worry about—David probably wasn't used to doing the hard physical labor of building a house. That seemed plausible—until David died a few months later.

After David's death, a cardiac specialist informed me that if your arms or legs fall asleep when your body is at rest, that's the first sign of cardiac trouble. It means the heart is not functioning properly.

The heart is regulated by electricity. Isn't it likely that a massive electric jolt would upset the body's electrical system and perhaps trigger cardiac arrhythmia? I share this theory with another doctor today, and he validates my hypothesis.

What is it about grieving that makes it so much easier to believe completely illogical reasons for a death, reasons that mean you're an accomplice to murder, rather than a completely logical reason that leaves you blameless?

❧

False guilt requires the awareness
that one has not caused hurt to others
but may have actually suffered the hurt
one thinks one has caused.

PAUL FERRINI

Aurora Winter

Yale: On Death

In his English class, Yale competed to get the topic of his choice, which was: Death. As I put the finishing touches on this manuscript, inserting quotes from others, he compiles a booklet of his own, a collection of ten poems on the subject of death.

Yale notes that "Hills of Blue" is his favorite poem, "I really love that poem because I wrote it, obviously. And because I think it is hopeful and interesting to think about eternal life and a heaven, or a non-earthly place where your soul was born. And how our existence might not only be based just on what we do here on earth, but rather on a compilation of all we do throughout our lives."

Hills of Blue

When limbs fail, and skin curls and screams,
You fall unto your grave, and into your dreams.

But it is only a stop in your path,
As through your eyes your life will flash,

All the moments which you once held so dear,
And your soul has now left, and you have no fear.

Rolling clouds, and hills of blue,
Now you're at home, where up you grew.

So leave behind your body, and enter this plane
And now it all makes sense, and all is sane.

For the torment you came, but now all is peace.
And unto your soul only one more crease.

YALE WINTER, AGE 16

Aurora Winter

Footprints on My Heart

His death has left its mark on me. What once was a raw wound healed and became a scar. What once was a scar healed and became footprints on my heart. I treasure those footprints. I'm never alone.

His life—his death—forever changed me. Who would I be without his life—and his death? What would chocolate be without bitter cacao and sugar? What would music be without notes and silences between? What would a rainbow be without rain and sun?

I see now that there can be no love without loss, no joy without sorrow, no peaks without valleys.

A flat, monotonous plain is not for me. I love the mountains and the babbling brooks that rush from dizzying heights down to the unfathomably deep sea.

I choose love—though it is entwined with loss.

I choose joy—though it is entwined with sorrow.

I choose peaks—though they are entwined with valleys.

I choose life—though it is entwined with death.

Life, glorious life! To embrace and savor each moment, to soothe one soul in torment, to inspire one discouraged friend, to be a warm wind under my son's wings, to leave my *own* footprints on hearts—that's all there is—and all I need to make my life worthwhile.

Struggling and Soaring with Angels

&

Out of suffering have emerged the strongest souls;
the most massive characters are seared with scars.

EDWIN CHAPIN

Aurora Winter

P.S. Laughter

As I read these notes, I'm struck by a new reaction. I actually laugh out loud, finding humor in some of my reactions, in much the same way that a horror movie may not be funny while you're gripped in its spell, but afterwards, when you know that it's a mouse and not a madman that has terrorized the heroine, it can be somewhat comic. Afterwards, you review the movie and think the special effects weren't *that* realistic, that it wasn't really *that* scary, that the plot had some holes that were ludicrously illogical.

Mind you, when you were under the movie's spell you weren't faking it when you nearly jumped right out of your skin as the madman's axe chopped through the bathroom door. No, you weren't faking it.

But, afterwards, when you know how everything turns out, when the lights come up and the curtains close and you're back in mundane reality, you can laugh. It was an emotional roller coaster — but already it doesn't seem quite real. You laugh because there were some parts that, viewed in a certain light, were absurd. You laugh at yourself.

Most of all, you laugh with relief because you're no longer enthralled by the movie's spell of terror, you're no longer seeing Death lurking around every corner.

You laugh with the joy of being alive, you laugh as you step out into the sunshine, you laugh because you're finally freed from Death's chilly shadow. Life is sweet again. What a great feeling!

Struggling and Soaring with Angels

&

I knew only one thing—which I have learned well by now:
love goes very far beyond the physical being of the beloved.
It finds its deepest meaning in his spiritual being, his inner self.
Whether or not he is actually present, whether or not he is still
alive at all, ceases somehow to be of importance.

VICTOR FRANKL

Aurora Winter

Prayer

Lord, make me an instrument of Your peace.
Where there is hatred, let me sow love;
Where there is injury, pardon;
Where there is doubt, faith;
Where there is despair, hope;
Where there is darkness, light;
And where there is sadness, joy;
O Divine Master, grant that I may not so much seek
To be consoled as to console;
To be understood as to understand;
To be loved as to love;
For it is in giving that we receive;
It is in pardoning that we are pardoned;
And it is in dying to self that we are born to eternal light.

ST. FRANCIS OF ASSISI

&

Struggling and Soaring with Angels

Aurora Winter

Stumbling Towards Ecstasy
Embracing an Open Heart

Soul Mate

If I wrote what happened in a movie, no one would believe it. I barely believe it myself. To describe the situation sounds outrageous—insane—rash. But to be here, inside my skin—rather than looking on from the outside— feels serene, safe, blissful. But I get ahead of myself. This is what happened.

Alex arrives at 3:15 pm. He wraps me in his arms and gives me the very first full-body hug we've ever shared. In that instant, I *know* that I love him. Without any reservation, I love him absolutely, completely, from the depths of my soul, with every fiber of my being. I feel that I have always loved him, that we are *reuniting*.

It feels as if we were lovers torn apart in some brutal war in a distant land. I'd lost all hope of ever seeing him again, lost all hope that he was even alive. And now, against all probabilities of time and space, we're together again. My heart overflows with joy, humbled by this incredible miracle.

It's an odd experience when he kisses me for the very first time. When my eyes are open, I see a stranger. Yet when we kiss, his lips, his tongue, his body all feel so *familiar*. I melt into him. He feels like home.

Struggling and Soaring with Angels

Instead of flirtatious banter, Alex and I tell each other the Truth. It's an amazingly honest and profound conversation. He really is extraordinary.

I've never had anything happen like this before, but I feel such a strong sense that we are reuniting that I want to make love. It's not coming from lust, but a deep desire to reconnect. I ask him if it's safe to surrender to him.

He doesn't answer my question with words, but pours love out through his eyes. His eyes flood me with such a divine, loving, healing, holy light. I've never experienced anything like it before. After a long time, the fear in me evaporates. I feel incredibly loved and cherished.

"I'd never want to hurt you. But 'safe' depends upon expectations." Alex asks, "What are your expectations?"

"I don't have an expectations."

He presses me, "What are your hopes? What are your dreams?"

I can't believe the words that fall out of my mouth. "I want to be with you until I die—or you die."

For a moment, we're *both* stunned. I don't know if I'm more astonished by the words I blurted out, or by the fact that that is honestly how I feel. I want to take back those reckless words, but cannot deny the truth.

I feel fear rising like a tidal wave in Alex. He tells me that freedom is the most important thing in the world to him. He reveals that he's like a hummingbird. He changes directions quickly, and needs to be free to follow his heart. He tells me that he doesn't want to "settle down." He doesn't want to have kids, get married or even live with anyone. He's afraid of being caged.

"Are you scared by what I said?" Alex asks.

His vehement declaration of independence should have felt like a bucket of ice water. But his honesty felt

Aurora Winter

good. I realize that my heart still feels peaceful, serene, blissful. I choose to trust my heart and surrender to this unwavering sense of knowing. I reply, "No. I love hummingbirds. And a caged hummingbird would die."

Reassured, he asks me how David died. I tell him everything, crying as I relive it. I feel seen and heard and loved.

He tells me that I have the purest heart he has ever seen. He's amazed by my devotion.

I'm happy to realize that I have something to teach this amazing being.

"Are you disappointed that I didn't say the same thing?" he asks.

"What same thing?" I ask.

"To be together forever."

I laugh. "It's a good thing that you didn't! It was scary enough when I said it."

Alex grins.

Satisfied that we understand each other, we stop talking with words. We communicate with our lips and tongues and bodies. I've never before experienced love-making as such a holy encounter. Our bodies connect, our souls connect, our hearts connect. Most intense of all is the connection between our eyes.

Joy. Rapture. Bliss. Ecstasy.

Peace. A peace beyond all understanding.

Struggling and Soaring with Angels

&

Love, and you shall be loved.

RALPH WALDO EMERSON

Aurora Winter

A Final Note from the Author About

Stumbling Towards Ecstasy
Embracing an Open Heart

Space does not permit me to reveal all the extraordinary events that preceded this day, nor the awesome and astonishing days that followed, which are the subject of *Stumbling Towards Ecstasy*. However, I don't want to leave you wondering if I regretted what happened on July 27.

Choosing an open heart involves risk. And on this day, I took a risk. I took it because—although it defied all logic—my heart was peaceful and clear.

Choosing to love and be loved always involves risk. And it involves rewards. Although many times I was afraid, choosing an open heart was the best decision I ever made.

It's the best decision anyone can ever make. Choosing to embrace love, in spite of the risk of having my heart broken, brought me the greatest gift life has to offer—true love.

&

When love beckons to you, follow him,
Though his ways are hard and steep,
And when his wings enfold you yield to him,
Though the sword hidden
among his pinions may wound you.
And when he speaks to you, believe in him.

KAHLIL GIBRAN

Struggling and Soaring with Angels

Acknowledgments

Many angels helped me soar in countless ways. Many angels invested their time, talent, and resources to help you soar, too. I'd like to take this opportunity to acknowledge a few of these earthly angels:

Raymond Aaron, Patrice Apodaca, Jeff & Debara Bailey,
Don & Doreen Ball, Gerard & Melanie Ball,
Mike & Danielle Ball, Cindy Bell, Kenton Beshore, Sue Bravo,
Cynthia Brian, Joy Burrows, Julie Castiglia, Lisa & Phil Case,
Sylvia Del Valle Garcia, Sarah Drislane, Eleanor Dugan,
Dr. Wayne Dyer, Janna Gelfand, Lee Gaither, Paul Gertz,
Gretchen Grace, Mark Victor Hansen, Rae Hatherton,
Louise Hay, Manny Hidalgo, Sheryl Ramstad Hvass,
Laurie Beth Jones, Jane Kelly, Joel Kotkin, Michael Kraus,
Annie & Ken Lindt, Teri March, Ross McDonald,
Seaton McLean, Paul Nagle, Anne Pellegrini, Beth Picariello,
Rick Reiff, Dr. Rachel Naomi Remen, Joel Roberts,
Tricia Rodewald, Bart Smith, Norman Sobel, Dr. Lo Sprague,
Stuart Tenzer, Brahm Wenger, Oprah Winfrey,
Dr. George Winter, Dr. Calvin Winter,
and—last but never least—Yale Winter.

Aurora Winter

Heart-felt thanks for contributions from:

Bryce Winter,
for being by my side through thick and thin,
and for overall design & event planning,
www.jetsetevent.com;
Dorothy Lawton,
for always believing in me and for being
my mother, my champion, and my coach,
http://consumerdirect.momsmakemore.com;
Alex Carroll,
for being on my wavelength, www.RadioPublicity.com;
Dr. Wayne Dyer,
for your blessing, www.drwaynedyer.com;
Bonnie Munster,
for connecting hearts, www.munsterandsons.com
David R. Hawkins,
for clarity, www.VeritasPub.com
Yousef Khanfar,
for capturing the divine light, www.YousefKhanfar.com;
Russell Friedman,
for your love and support
and for workshops that heal broken hearts
The Grief Recovery Institute, www.Grief-Recovery.com.

Struggling and Soaring with Angels

Recommended Reading

Tuesdays with Morrie by Mitch Albom
A New Path to the Waterfall by Raymond Carver
The Seven Spiritual Laws of Success by Deepak Chopra
There's a Spiritual Solution to Every Problem by Wayne Dyer
Embraced by the Light by Betty Eadie
Man's Search for Meaning by Victor Frankl
The Prophet by Kahlil Gibran
You Can Heal Your Life by Louise Hay
Power versus Force by David R. Hawkins
The Grief Recovery Handbook by John James and
Russell Friedman
When Children Grieve by John James, Russell Friedman and
Leslie Matthews
Traveling Mercies by Anne Lamott
A Grief Observed by C. S. Lewis
My Grandfather's Blessings by Rachel Naomi Remen
The Four Agreements by Don Miguel Ruiz
A Return to Love by Marianne Williamson

Aurora Winter

About the Author

Aurora Winter is a film and television producer and award-winning screenwriter. She has worked as an executive for film and television companies in Los Angeles, Toronto, and London.

Aurora has been interviewed on radio and television, and was the subject of a half-hour television documentary featuring her work as a writer. She has been profiled in numerous national and international magazines and newspapers.

Aurora is currently living and writing *Stumbling towards Ecstasy: Embracing an Open Heart*, the sequel to this book.

Media: Radio, TV and Print

For more information, visit www.AuroraWinter.com. To schedule an interview, please call 866-344-3108.

Struggling and Soaring with Angels

Comments?

I'd welcome your feedback, comments, or questions. I'd appreciate hearing if this book has helped you move forward in your own life. I'd be honored to hear your story of loss, healing, and transformation. You can contact me at the address below.

Aurora Winter
c/o Dandelion Sky Press,
1280 Bison, Suite B9-40, Newport Beach, CA 92660
email: DandelionSkyPr@aol.com
Or visit: www.AuroraWinter.com

Speaking Engagements

Aurora speaks passionately about living life to the fullest, no matter what. To book Aurora as a speaker, call 866-344-3108 toll free.

Special Sales

Books are available at special quantity discounts for fund-raising, educational use, charities, promotions, and premiums. A beautiful 48-page booklet containing selected pages from this book is also available.

Struggling and Soaring with Angels:
Healing a Broken Heart
by Aurora Winter

Complete Book: ISBN 0-9722497-8-8
Booklet (48-page excerpt) ISBN 0-9722497-7-X.
To order, phone 866-344-3108 toll free

The sequel,

Stumbling Towards Ecstasy:
Embracing an Open Heart
by Aurora Winter

is scheduled for publication Summer 2004. Order your special signed first edition now.

Order on-line at:
www.AuroraWinter.com

ORDER FORM

FAX ORDERS: (866) 344-3107 toll free

MAIL ORDERS: Dandelion Sky Press
1280 Bison, Suite B9-40 Newport Beach, CA 92660

PHONE ORDERS: (866) 344-3108 please have your credit card ready.

EMAIL ORDERS: DandelionSkyPr@aol.com

Struggling and Soaring with Angels   **$14.95 each**
Book (softcover)
Quantity desired: _____

Struggling and Soaring with Angels: Excerpt   **$4.95 each**
Booklet (48 pages)
Quantity desired: _____

** PREORDER SPECIAL SIGNED FIRST EDITION **

Stumbling Towards Ecstasy
Hardcover Book. Scheduled publication date: Summer 2004   **$24.95 each**
Quantity desired: _____

Stumbling Towards Ecstasy
Softcover Book. Scheduled publication date: Fall 2004   **$14.95 each**
Quantity desired: _____

- -

SHIPPING AND HANDLING

US: Book(s): $3.95 for each book and $1.95 for each additional book.
Booklet(s) $2.95 for the first booklet and $.95 for each additional booklet.

SALES TAX: Please add 7.5% for products shipped to California addresses.

PAYMENT: Check enclosed (payable to Dandelion Sky Press) or Credit Card:

☐ Visa   ☐ Mastercard
☐ AMEX   ☐ Discover

Card number: _____

Name on card: _____ Expiry Date: _____

Name: _____

Address: _____

Phone: _____

Email address: _____

Or order online!
www.AuroraWinter.com

ORDER FORM

FAX ORDERS: (866) 344-3107 toll free

MAIL ORDERS: Dandelion Sky Press
1280 Bison, Suite B9-40 Newport Beach, CA 92660

PHONE ORDERS: (866) 344-3108 please have your credit card ready.

EMAIL ORDERS: DandelionSkyPr@aol.com

Struggling and Soaring with Angels   **$14.95 each**
Book (softcover)
Quantity desired: _____

Struggling and Soaring with Angels: Excerpt   **$4.95 each**
Booklet (48 pages)
Quantity desired: _____

** PREORDER SPECIAL SIGNED FIRST EDITION **

Stumbling Towards Ecstasy
Hardcover Book. Scheduled publication date: Summer 2004 **$24.95 each**
Quantity desired: _____

Stumbling Towards Ecstasy
Softcover Book. Scheduled publication date: Fall 2004   **$14.95 each**
Quantity desired: _____

- -

SHIPPING AND HANDLING

US: Book(s): $3.95 for each book and $1.95 for each additional book.
Booklet(s) $2.95 for the first booklet and $.95 for each additional booklet.

SALES TAX: Please add 7.5% for products shipped to California addresses.

PAYMENT: Check enclosed (payable to Dandelion Sky Press) or Credit Card:

☐ Visa   ☐ Mastercard
☐ AMEX   ☐ Discover

Card number: _____

Name on card: _____ Expiry Date: _____

Name: _____

Address: _____

Phone: _____

Email address: _____

Or order online!
www.AuroraWinter.com

ORDER FORM

FAX ORDERS: (866) 344-3107 toll free

MAIL ORDERS: Dandelion Sky Press
1280 Bison, Suite B9-40 Newport Beach, CA 92660

PHONE ORDERS: (866) 344-3108 please have your credit card ready.

EMAIL ORDERS: DandelionSkyPr@aol.com

Struggling and Soaring with Angels   **$14.95 each**
Book (softcover)
Quantity desired: _____

Struggling and Soaring with Angels: Excerpt   **$4.95 each**
Booklet (48 pages)
Quantity desired: _____

** PREORDER SPECIAL SIGNED FIRST EDITION **

Stumbling Towards Ecstasy
Hardcover Book. Scheduled publication date: Summer 2004 **$24.95 each**
Quantity desired: _____

Stumbling Towards Ecstasy
Softcover Book. Scheduled publication date: Fall 2004   **$14.95 each**
Quantity desired: _____

- -

SHIPPING AND HANDLING

US: Book(s): $3.95 for each book and $1.95 for each additional book.
Booklet(s) $2.95 for the first booklet and $.95 for each additional booklet.

SALES TAX: Please add 7.5% for products shipped to California addresses.

PAYMENT: Check enclosed (payable to Dandelion Sky Press) or Credit Card:

☐ Visa   ☐ Mastercard
☐ AMEX   ☐ Discover

Card number: _____

Name on card: _____ Expiry Date: _____

Name: _____

Address: _____

Phone: _____

Email address: _____

Or order online!
www.AuroraWinter.com